6.31

R. H Cricks

A

M

BOOK REVIEW

"Lighting for Photography." By W. Nurnberg. *Focal Press, 12s. 6d.*

THIS is one of the best books I have read on modern lighting for photographers. The author knows his subject and can explain theory and practice in clear and practical language. Many diagrams and over 100 photographs by first-class American and European photographers show the reader the many styles of lighting in use to-day.

Starting with chapters on the theory of light and emulsions, the practical means of using them are described. An interesting chapter on electricity is contributed by our B.K.S. secretary, Mr. Cricks, who also points out the rules for safety so often neglected by photographers. Types of lighting units are described in detail, with suggestions for economical installations for different classes of studios. The fundamentals of lights and lighting are emphasised in simple language, with diagrams and photographs to help visualise the various points.

It is chiefly the chapters on portraiture of the face and figure that will appeal to kine. cameramen. In addition, the methods of dealing with glassware, leatherware, fabrics, etc., will prove instructive. The range of subjects dealt with is unusually wide for this type of book and even experienced photographers will find useful hints.

The author has a definite photographic style of his own but shows many other examples by well-known workers so that the reader can exercise his personal taste. On page 64 Mr. Nurnberg advises the reader to use back-projection as sparingly as possible; he suggests it is overrated and only suitable for cheap work. From experience, I suspect the real reason is not bad art but bad technique. The examples of perfect background projection in many films show that, given the right equipment, a first-class cameraman can produce results to satisfy the most captious critic.

There are very few statements in the book which can be challenged and I have no hesitation in advising cameramen to invest 12s. 6d. in a copy.

L.I.

B.K.S. JOURNAL,
JAN. 1941

LIGHTING FOR PHOTOGRAPHY

Printed and bound in Great Britain by Richard Clay and Company, Ltd., Bungay, Suffolk.
Illustrations printed by Hunt, Barnard & Company, Ltd., Aylesbury, Buckinghamshire.

LIGHTING FOR PHOTOGRAPHY

MEANS AND METHODS

WALTER NURNBERG

THE FOCAL PRESS

LONDON and NEW YORK

CONTENTS

4

Mu 4/18/73

5

Photography is a combination of artistic and technical manipulations. Accordingly, photographers almost invariably show in their inclinations, preferences and efforts, a split into two camps.

Some of them look upon their craft as an art, are deeply interested in its pictorial possibilities and aesthetic theories, but get reserved if it comes to discussing the more sober aspects of technique. Others of the opposite creed have often only a smile for such enthusiasts, but the more intensely devote themselves to never-ending technical experiments and scientific problems.

The writer on photographic matters and his editor never know to which of these two camps their readers will belong, whether they will frown at every diagram or be impatient of any sentence of speculative implications. The obvious solution of the problem is to " translate " anything you want to say into the commonsense language of the practical man, make your technical diagrams pictorially convincing and choose pictorial illustrations as clear cut as a scientific drawing.

There is nothing new in this method. It has been applied again and again to popular demonstrations of many kinds. It is new in one respect as it appears in this book : it tries to take the reader quite a bit farther with our subject than publications of a more elementary type have hitherto undertaken to do.

We have not confined ourselves to telling merely " where to put your lamps ", but have tried to go back to the technical roots of artificial lighting, to discuss the advantages and limitations of the different light sources, to sketch the principles of their practical use and give suggestions as to their individual application.

Neither do we attempt to win addicts to any lighting system by claiming infallibility for the working style of some master photographer. Anybody can see that the photographic handwriting of the author is a very definite one, but his pictures have been carefully balanced by outstanding examples of other workers on both sides of the Atlantic, in order to prove how manifold and impressive are the styles and varieties of photographic lighting, whether it be called graphic, romantic, naturalistic, functional, dramatic or what else you prefer.

Meanwhile, author and publishers would like to express their thanks to Mr. R. Howard Cricks, F.R.P.S., for his contributions to the technical chapters, and to Mr. R. B. Ling for reading the manuscript and the proofs on behalf of the author, who, while in His Majesty's service, was unable to follow his book through the press.

A. KRASZNA-KRAUSZ

The Focal Press, November 1940

7

KEY TO LIGHTING DIAGRAMS

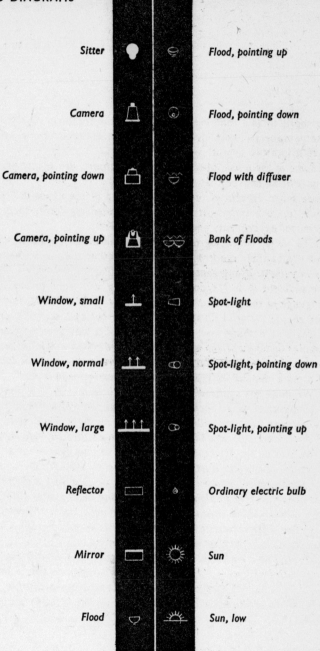

Sitter		Flood, pointing up
Camera		Flood, pointing down
Camera, pointing down		Flood with diffuser
Camera, pointing up		Bank of Floods
Window, small		Spot-light
Window, normal		Spot-light, pointing down
Window, large		Spot-light, pointing up
Reflector		Ordinary electric bulb
Mirror		Sun
Flood		Sun, low

I

THE THEORY OF LIGHT

B

LIGHT AND THE PHOTOGRAPHIC EMULSION

A more apt definition of the word photography than the etymological "writing with light" would be *painting with light*. If light is our paint, and the sensitive emulsion our canvas, then it is necessary, before one can become a master of the craft, to investigate the nature of these materials; for while the outdoor photographer finds his paint ready mixed for him by the sun, the indoor worker, like the old masters, has to mix it himself.

Upon his knowledge of its ingredients will depend the success of his work.

LIGHT—WHAT IT IS

Visible light forms a very small proportion—less than one octave—of an enormous gamut, totalling about twenty octaves, of so-called *electro-magnetic waves*, which permeate space, and which travel at the incredible velocity of 186,300 miles per second. The distance from the crest of one wave to the crest of the next is called the *wave-length*, a term which radio has made familiar to us all, and which is mathematically linked with the *frequency*.

The wave-lengths of this enormous range of waves are measured in terms of the *micron* (μ) which equals $\frac{1}{1000}$ mm.; the *millimicron* ($\mu\mu$), or millionth of a millimetre; or the Ångström unit (Å or ÅU), which is equal to one ten-millionth of a millimetre; and in the other direction, in ascending units to thousands of metres. Only vibrations of a wave-length between 4000 and 7000 Å (400 to 700 $\mu\mu$ or 0·4 to 0·7 μ) are perceptible to the eye, and these, together with the neighbouring infra-red and ultra-violet rays, are termed *light*.

THE VISIBLE SPECTRUM

It is necessary to consider rather more closely that band of wave-lengths known as the visible spectrum.

If we pass a beam of sunlight through a prism and then intercept the light thus transmitted, we shall observe, not a white patch of light, but a light-beam which has been broken up into a continuous band of different colours like a rainbow. This band, which we call the *spectrum*, includes an infinite number of hues, ranging from crimson red—which is least bent by the prism—to violet,

10

which is refracted at the most oblique angle. The principal hues in between the crimson-red and the violet are: vermilion-red, orange, yellow, green and blue.

Besides these visible vibrations, two other kinds of *invisible* rays are contained in that compound which makes up "white light": ultra-violet and infra-red rays. Although these two radiations are not visible to the naked eye, and are therefore called the invisible spectrum, they can under certain conditions be registered by photographic emulsions. (See p. 14.)

THE COLOUR OF LIGHT

We now see that "white light" is in reality nothing but a conglomeration of the different colours contained in the spectrum *plus* ultra-violet (wave-lengths under 4000 ÅU) and infra-red (wave-lengths over 7000 ÅU).

To simplify the matter *we may divide the visible spectrum into three bands: the blue band; the green band; the red band.*

The principal components of the three colour-bands are as follows:

    In the blue band
          violet with a wave-length of 4000 to 4500 ÅU.
          blue   ,,   ,,   4500 ,, 5000 ÅU.
    In the green band
          green with a wave-length of 5000 to 5600 ÅU.
          yellow   ,,   ,,   5600 ,, 5900 ÅU.
    In the red band
          orange with a wave-length of 5900 to 6400 ÅU.
          red   ,,   ,,   6400 ,, 7200 ÅU.

It must be clearly understood that the above-mentioned colours do not stand well defined " side by side " in the spectrum, but that they are connected and blended into each other by further intermediate colours, hues which are mixtures of each of the neighbouring colours. For instance, there are several shades of blue-violet between blue and violet, several shades of blue-green between blue and green, and so forth.

Blue, green and red are called primary colours because with them any other colour may be synthetised. If one mixes *the three primary colours in equal quantities, white light will be produced.* Midday sunlight is thus white light because it contains the three colour wave-bands in equal proportions.

It is only logical that if these proportions are altered the colour of the light too will be altered. For instance, light produced by our electric bulbs, although still being a kind of "white light", is actually much more red than the light produced by noon sunlight. The reason for this is that approximately 50% of this light is transmitted on the red wave-band, 30% on the green wave-band and only 20% on the blue wave-band—provided the bulb is being burnt at its normal voltage. (See p. 30.)

If such an alteration of the proportions of the different colour-bands in the spectrum makes a clearly visible difference in the colour impression, it is obvious that one can produce any desired colour if one succeeds in getting rid more or less of certain colours contained in the spectrum. In short, a given colour is the result of having omitted some other colours (or colour) from the complete spectrum.

Any colour can be abstracted from white light by the use of a transparent medium of suitable colour. Thus, to remove the surplus red from the light of our ordinary electric bulb, we have to use a screen which will abstract red; reference to the table of colour-bands (on p. 11) will suggest that such a screen must transmit violet, blue, green and yellow. In effect, such a screen (or filter) would be blue-green in colour, and since this colour abstracts red, *blue-green* is known as *minus-red*, and red and blue-green, which together make up white light, are known as *complementary colours*.

Similarly, a mixture of blue-violet and red-orange, or magenta, will intercept the green rays, and consequently *magenta* is known as *minus-green*. A mixture of green, yellow, orange and red will abstract blue, and consequently *yellow* is known as *minus-blue*. Green and magenta are complementary colours, and so are blue and yellow.

THE EFFECT OF COLOUR ON THE NEGATIVE

In ordinary monochrome photography, colours are replaced by different degrees of brightness between white and black. As a matter of fact, the brightness of the colours can be estimated by their reflection coefficients.

Orange reflects, for example, approximately 62%, green approximately 25%, blue-green approximately 15%, vermilion approximately 15%, cobalt blue approximately 15%, ultramarine blue approximately 12%.

These figures, however, have not much practical importance for the photographer, as there is not yet a photographic negative material available which "sees" colours as does the human eye. Moreover, almost every type of negative material registers colours in its own particular way. The *colour sensitivity* of our plates and films is everything but uniform.

The colour sensitivity of an emulsion is expressed in terms of wave-lengths, and is in practice illustrated by means of *wedge spectrograms*, which, although they may look highly abstruse, actually illustrate graphically the sensitivity of the emulsion to the various wave-lengths of light. A number of these spectrograms relating to different types of emulsions are reproduced; it will be seen that the figures along the scale represent the wave-length (in hundreds of Ångströms), and the height of the spectrogram at any point represents the sensitivity of the emulsion to light of that wave-length.

While many practical photographers are apt to regard such data as mere scientific curiosities, it is well worth while mastering their meaning. Even in relatively unscientific matters, such as portraiture, they will enable one to answer questions as to how the colour of the sitter's dress will reproduce;

12

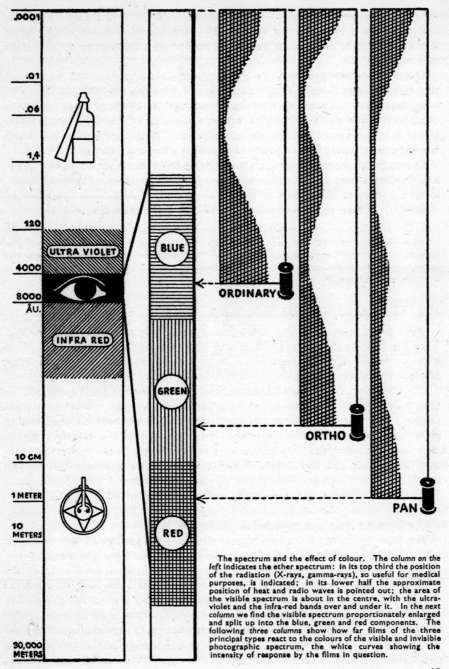

The spectrum and the effect of colour. The *column on the left* indicates the ether spectrum: in its top third the position of the radiation (X-rays, gamma-rays), so useful for medical purposes, is indicated; in its lower half the approximate position of heat and radio waves is pointed out; the area of the visible spectrum is about in the centre, with the ultra-violet and the infra-red bands over and under it. In the *next column* we find the visible spectrum proportionately enlarged and split up into the blue, green and red components. The following *three columns* show how far films of the three principal types react to the colours of the visible and invisible photographic spectrum, the white curves showing the intensity of response by the films in question.

they are of immense value in making an intelligent use of filters (see p. 15) and of different light sources (see p. 28)—particularly of recently developed types whose light emission is restricted to certain very narrow bands in the spectrum.

The *ordinary* old-type negative material registers blue—for the human eye the darkest colour—as the lightest; this will be apparent from p. 13. This exaggeration of the blue is in fact so great that an ordinary plate or film is completely blind to the difference between the blue of the sky and the white of the clouds. Other colours are not registered at all, not even those which the eye perceives as the brightest, *i.e.*, green, yellow and orange.

The negative materials which are sensitive from violet up to yellow-green and also for a part of the ultra-violet are generally known as *orthochromatic;* those sensitive to all colours of the visible spectrum plus ultra-violet as *panchromatic.* The extension of sensitivity is clear from their spectrograms.

Modern science is even able to produce negative materials sensitive to the vibrations of the *invisible* spectrum; one kind responds exclusively to ultra-violet rays down to wave-length of 1200 Å, another to infra-red rays up to 10,000 Å (heat waves). The usefulness of these two latter negative materials has so far been strictly limited to certain specialised fields of scientific and outdoor photography.

THE REPRODUCTION OF COLOURS

We have already seen that the *ordinary* material is practically colour-blind. The only colours it does see, violet and blue, are misrepresented to such an extent that this ordinary negative material is useful only for the reproduction of black-and-white objects.

The colour-sensitiveness of *orthochromatic* emulsions has been extended, so that they register also green, yellow-green and often also yellow to a small degree. The orthochromatic materials are still predominantly susceptible to violet and blue. There is therefore—quite apart from the fact that orthochromatic materials are blind to orange and red—still a divergence between our own vision and the vision of the camera. In order to overcome this divergence we must use a *filter* (see p. 15) which absorbs the superfluous influx of ultra-violet, violet and blue light without losing anything of the yellow-green.

Panchromatic materials register all colours.

We have to distinguish, however, between two groups of panchromatic stock. While the first (older) group renders red far too light, the second group (sometimes called ortho-panchromatic) reproduces red approximately correctly. Neither type, however, has the exaggerated sensitivity to green of the human eye; should we therefore desire to adjust the colour perception of panchromatic materials to that of our vision, we have again to make use of suitable *filters* (see p. 15). With normal panchromatic material we shall have to use a green filter in order to lose a high percentage of the incident blue simultaneously with a smaller portion of the red. With ortho-panchromatic

14

stock a yellow filter might be sufficient, red not being excessively stressed by this kind of emulsion.

One thing will be apparent from the foregoing remarks: that, while ordinary and orthochromatic emulsions have their applications for certain types of work, for normal photographic work *panchromatic emulsions have the most advantages*.

As we shall see later, panchromatic emulsions, in combination with various filters, make it not only possible to register a colour-impression at its true value, but also to " fake " the colours of the object according to our will. This "faking", or exaggeration of colour differences, is, for instance, most helpful when reproducing coloured patterns in which the colours have the same tone-values, and where it is therefore necessary to create an artificial contrast in order to avoid a grey, colourless effect and to inform the spectator that there were different colours on the original.

LIGHT FILTERS

As far as black-and-white work in artificial light is concerned, the principal applications of filters are to improve the rendering of colours, and to obtain a more natural scale of brightnesses, in which case the filter is known as a *correcting filter;* or to increase the difference in rendering of various colours, in which case the filter is known as a *contrast filter.*

A light filter can be put either directly in front of the lens, or directly in front of the light source. In either case the colour medium is usually dyed gelatine; for use on the light source it is generally mounted in a frame, or just slipped into slots provided on the lamp housing.

In filters intended to be used on the lens, the gelatine is usually cemented between two pieces of optical glass, and mounted in a ring clipping to the lens mount. Lens filters must receive the same careful treatment as the lens itself.

As we have already learnt (see p. 12), the term " complementary colour " describes that colour which produces white light when mixed with the colour (or colours) to which it is complementary. For instance : red complements blue-green, yellow-green complements violet, yellow complements indigo.

From this it follows that the beam of " white light," after having been transmitted through a flat piece of coloured glass or coloured gelatine, takes on the colour of the transmitting medium intercepting it. The reason for this is that *only those light-rays have been transmitted through the light-filter which are not complementary to its own colour, while the complementary colours have been partially or totally absorbed by it.*

A *deep orange filter* e.g. transmits freely only that part of the colour wave-band which lies between 5900 Å and infra-red, *i.e.,* deep yellow, orange, vermilion, crimson red and infra-red. Rays of a wave-length between 5800 and 5500 Å (*i.e.,* yellow to yellow-green) are progressively absorbed towards the lower wave-length, while the remaining part of the spectrum, from green to ultra-violet is, for all practical purposes, fully absorbed. Light filtered through an orange filter will render a blue and a green object darker, while red is rendered slightly and yellow considerably lighter. (This and similar information is based on the assumption that a panchromatic material is being used.)

Visual Colour	Filter No. Wratten	Ilford	Filter Factor Ortho-Pan	Pan	Colours rendered darker	Colours unaltered	Colours rendered lighter
Very deep Red	88	207	—	—	—	—	Infra-red
Dark Red	29 (F)	205	7	4	All except Red	—	Red
Red	26 25 (A)	204	4	4	Violet, Blue, Green, Yellow	Orange	Red
Light Red	23 (E) 22 (E2)	—	$3\frac{1}{2}$	$3\frac{1}{2}$	Violet, Blue, Green, Yellow	—	Orange and Red
Orange	21 16 (T)	202 201	2	2	Violet, Blue, Green	Yellow	Orange and Red
Deep Yellow	15 (G) 9 (K3)	111 110 109	$1\frac{1}{2}$–2	$1\frac{3}{4}$–$2\frac{1}{2}$	Violet, Blue	Green	Yellow, Orange, Red
Yellow	8 (K2) 5 (Aero 2) 3 (Aero 1)	108 107 106	$1\frac{1}{2}$	$1\frac{1}{2}$	Violet, Blue	Blue-green	Green, Yellow, Orange, Red
Light Yellow	7 (K1½) 6 (K1)	105 104 101 103	$1\frac{1}{4}$–$1\frac{1}{2}$	$1\frac{1}{4}$–$1\frac{1}{2}$	Violet	Blue	Green, Yellow, Orange, Red
Yellow-green	56 (B3)	402	$3\frac{1}{2}$	$3\frac{1}{2}$	Violet, Red	Blue, Orange	Green, Yellow
Green	57 (B2) 55	404 405	6–7	8–9	Violet, Blue, Orange, Red	Yellow	Green
Light Blue-green	38	403	3	3	Orange, Red	Violet, Yellow	Blue, Green
Dark Blue-green	44a	303	15	15	Yellow, Orange, Red	Violet	Blue, Green
Blue	49a (C4)	304	—	—	Yellow, Orange, Red	Violet, Green	Blue
Blue-violet	47 (C5) 48 (C2)	305	—	—	Yellow, Orange, Red	Blue-green	Violet, Blue
Purple	35 (D)	501	—	—	Green, Yellow, Orange	Blue	Violet, Red
Magenta	31	502	—	—	Green, Yellow	Violet	Blue, Orange, Red

This table shows the characteristics of the more generally used filters of the two manufactures: *Kodak* and *Ilford*. The filters grouped in each section, while not identical, have for most practical purposes similar characteristics within the visible spectrum. The filter factors (see p. 53) shown are for ortho-panchromatic and panchromatic emulsions, for exposure to tungsten-filament lighting (see p. 29). Where no filter factor is shown, a test should be made with the particular emulsion and illuminant to be employed, since the omission indicates that the factor may vary widely.

16

LIGHT AND THE SUBJECT

Light becomes visible and usable for photographic purposes only when it is intercepted by some substance and is reflected from it. Dust in the atmosphere is already sufficient to make light perceptible to vision. It follows that an object becomes visible only when it reflects the light which falls on it. This statement does not mean, however, that the object has to reflect the same amount of light as is caught by its surface; it is always a fact that only a certain part of the light is *reflected*, while the rest is *absorbed* or " sucked up ".

The lightness or darkness of a given surface depends mainly on two factors.

The first is the *quantity of light which is received* by it, this factor being governed by the brightness and intensity of the light source and by the distance of this light source from the object. *The efficacy of illumination is inversely proportional to the square of the distance.* Thus placing a lamp of 100 watts at a distance of 3 ft. from a given object (or screen) produces the same intensity of illumination as a lamp of 900 watts placed at a distance of 9 ft.

The second factor is the coefficient of reflection—meaning, in plain language, that *percentage of light which is reflected* from a surface.

PHOTOMETRIC UNITS

We thus have three quantities to consider in the measurement of light for photography: (1) *the total quantity of light emitted by the source;* (2) the *intensity* (not the quantity) *of light falling on the subject;* (3) *the intensity of light reflected back from the subject.*

(1) The accepted unit for all photometric units is the *international candle*—actually the light emitted by a candle made to very exact specifications. The emission of this source is the *candle-power* (c.p.).

(2) If we take a surface having an area of 1 sq. ft., and place it at a distance of 1 ft. from our candle, it will receive a total light flux of 1 *lumen*. The intensity of light falling on the surface will be 1 *foot-candle*.

Now, if we place our surface at a distance of 2 ft. from the source, it will, by the inverse-square law, receive only $\frac{1}{4}$ lumen of light, and will receive an intensity of only $\frac{1}{4}$ foot-candle. If, however, we take a surface of 4 sq. ft. and place it 2 ft. from the source, then it will receive again a total of 1 lumen; but the intensity will be unaltered at $\frac{1}{4}$ foot-candle.

(3) The reflection of light from an illuminated surface is measured by the *foot-lambert*. If our surface is 1 ft. from the source, and hence receives an illumination of 1 foot-candle, and

C   17 if, furthermore, we assume it to be a completely diffusing surface, with a reflectivity of, say, 90%, then the brightness of the surface will be 0·9 foot-lambert. As we shall shortly see, however, no surface is completely diffusing, and actually the reflection will vary according to the direction in which the measurement is taken.

REFLECTION

We have to distinguish between two main kinds of reflection: *concentrated or specular reflection* and *diffused reflection*.

Concentrated or specular reflection means that the light-beam which falls upon a surface is reflected back without being scattered.

Diffused reflection implies that the light-beam is broken up, or scattered in all directions, at the moment of incidence.

This classification describes only the most extreme effects of reflection, and there is, between these two antipodal types, a wide variety of " in-between " reflections which combine in themselves the properties of both extremes in varying degrees.

The extent to which a reflection is concentrated or diffused depends on the kind and structure of the reflecting surface. *The smoother and more highly polished that surface is, the more concentrated will be the reflection; the duller and more textural the surface, the more diffused will be the reflection.*

The ideal surfaces for producing a specular or concentrated reflection are provided by materials such as plate-glass mirrors, shiny and perfectly flat metal sheets, etc. On the other hand, surfaces such as white plaster walls, grainy, matt cardboards or white blotting-paper are the best bases for diffused reflections.

Materials such as glazed boards, matt metal surfaces—e.g., matted aluminium sheets, etc.—provide reflections which lie between the concentrated and the completely diffused reflection and which will demonstrate therefore, in a varying degree, a strongly marked direction of reflection while at the same time another part of the light-rays is freely dispersed.

In the case of specular reflection, the *angle of reflection is equal to the angle of incidence.* In order to make the implications of this clear, one just has to imagine a tennis ball being thrown to the ground at some angle or other. It will be observed—provided the ball has been thrown without a spin—that it rebounds at an angle which corresponds exactly with the angle of its incidence.

Actually the same law applies to the case of diffused reflection, but the beam of light is split up into so great a number of individual rays that the reflection is dispersed in all directions. As mentioned, there are instances where the greater part of the total amount of reflection is bounced back at the angle of incidence, while a smaller portion is scattered about haphazardly.

These considerations are of some practical consequence. They not only influence lighting technique, but also the choice of camera angle. This does *not* apply when we have to deal with a completely diffused reflection, as then

18

the light is split up and redistributed in all directions in equal proportions, thus producing an extensive field of even illumination which can be viewed from nearly every angle without altering its appearance.

But when we have to cope with a concentrated reflection we shall see that the direction of the reflected light-beam is strongly marked and the field of illumination strictly limited. If our camera is to register this concentrated reflection, it is essential that the concentrated, reflected light-beam is caught by the lens. It follows that, if the " width " of the reflection is only narrow, the lens must face, more or less, the direction from which the reflection is thrown.

The more we widen the angle between the line of reflection and the line of camera-vision, the less reflection will be registered on our negative.

ABSORPTION OF LIGHT

We have already heard that a surface never reflects the same amount of light as it receives, but that a certain amount of it is always absorbed. *The more light reflected the lighter will the surface appear; the less light reflected the darker will it seem.*

Unfortunately, our naked eye can only distinguish relative luminosities in a rather rough manner. Although we can say that one thing is lighter or darker than another when seeing them side by side, we are rather vague in our judgment of tone values; we can perceive the relation of one tone to another, but cannot exactly estimate the extent of it.

Everyone who has ever handled a camera knows how easy it is to be deceived in this respect, and everyone has been surprised to find a negative under- or over-exposed although at the time of exposure the lighting conditions might have seemed entirely reliable. The human eye has the wonderful faculty of being able to adapt itself only too willingly to changing lighting conditions, though it may need some time to adjust itself. Every photographer will have experienced how a comparatively weak light dazzles him when coming out of a dark-room and how consequently the brightness of the light gets easily over-valued.

Luckily once again science has come to the rescue of our erring judgment. Detailed information on the coefficient of reflection, relating to different kinds of surfaces, is available.

Apart from a mirror, which is only able to produce a concentrated reflection, the most strongly reflecting surface is provided by a block of chalk or a mass of magnesium carbonate; they are the " whitest " substances known, and reflect over 90% of the incident light. The next best reflecting materials are: white plaster with a coefficient of 90%, white blotting-paper with 80%, white matt paint with approximately 75%, glossy white paint with approximately 70%, white paper with between 60% and 80%, according to structure of its surface. Grey painted surfaces reflect between 20% and 60% of the incident light, the coefficient of reflection varying according to the tone-value. The darkest, most light-absorbent surface is black silk-velvet with a coefficient of only 0·3%. Matt-black paint on wood reflects more (approximately 3%); black paper or board up to 10%.

19

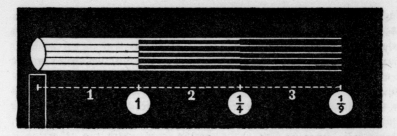

The efficacy of illumination is inversely proportional to the square of distance. Two yards away from the light source the efficacy of illumination is one-quarter of that one yard away, and three yards away it is only one-ninth of that one yard away.

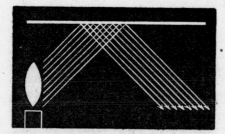

If the reflecting surface is smooth, the reflection will be sharply defined (concentrated, regular, specular reflection). In such a case the angle of incidence will be equal to the angle of reflection.

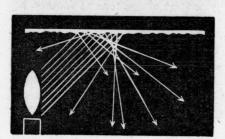

If the reflecting surface is coarse, the reflected beams will not be sharply defined (diffused reflection) and will be dispersed in all directions.

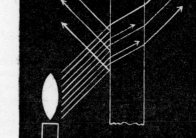

A transparent medium will partly reflect, partly absorb and partly refract the rays of light. The light is refracted, bent, as it enters from one medium of certain density into another medium of different density.

20

Knowledge of these facts comes in most handy in practice. They tell us, for instance—without the need of experiment—that, when photographing a piece of clean chalk on a sheet of white paper, the chalk will appear white on the photograph, while the paper background—having also appeared to our bare eye as white—is registered as a light grey on the photographic print. We are also informed by comparing the above-mentioned coefficients that—using the same quantity of light—we have to expose a sheet of black paper seven times as long as a sheet of white paper in order to obtain the same density on our negative, or the same effect of brightness on the print.

THE REFRACTION OF LIGHT

Until now we have only considered substances which do not transmit light, but merely absorb and reflect it. But as soon as we go a step further, and consider " transparencies "—glass, cellophane, celluloid, etc.—we become aware of yet another new phenomenon.

Light is refracted when it enters from one medium of a certain density into a medium of a different density, as from air into glass and *vice versa*. A light-ray falling upon a sheet of glass in the perpendicular is transmitted straight through it without being bent, while every light-ray meeting the surface at an angle other than 90° is deflected from its perpendicular course, the bend becoming more pronounced the more acute the angle of light-incidence. (The angle of refraction is further determined by the surface form of the " refractor ", e.g., a round glass will bend light differently from a plane glass sheet.)

The refracted light-beam after having entered the glass sheet travels straight through it—provided the glass substance is uniform all through—but, in the case of a flat sheet of glass, bends back into the direction of its incidence as soon as it leaves the glass and re-enters the less dense matter of air.

The outstanding application of refraction is, of course, the lens of our camera, which illustrates the fundamental law that, in the case of a transparent object having curved surfaces, light is refracted towards the thickest part of the object—that is to say, towards the centre of a convex lens. Exactly the same effect can be seen through a water-bottle.

A field of photography in which refraction is of the utmost consequence is the photography of glassware. (See p. 149.)

THE COLOUR OF OUR SUBJECTS

So far, we have concerned ourselves only with the colour of transparent substances or with the colour of light itself. In fact, the same basic laws which apply to transparent matter are also applicable to non-transparent (opaque) substances. The only difference is that instead of having to deal with trans-mission and absorption we now have to deal with reflection and absorption.

We have already seen the way in which opaque substances invariably reflect

21

and absorb light. *A surface therefore appears to us as coloured because it reflects a certain colour, while absorbing others in varying degrees.* Or, in other words, the white light is filtered, this time, however, by reflection, and not as before by transmission.

An object appears to us as red because it reflects only those rays of the incident white light which are red, while it absorbs those which are green and blue. Similarly an object is blue because it reflects blue light rays and absorbs the green, orange, red and, partially, the yellow components contained in the spectrum of the incident light. We describe an object as yellow when it reflects yellow, red and green in different proportions but absorbs blue; we describe it as green when it reflects green, blue-green and yellow but absorbs red, dark blue and violet.

It must now be realised that an object which appears to us as red, blue or green or as any other colour when seen under " white light ", will change its colour when illuminated by coloured light. If one goes to the extreme by illuminating a coloured object with its exact complementary colour—for instance, a blue-green dress with red light—the dress will look black. The reason for this is obvious. The filter introduced into the path of the incident white light-beam has absorbed practically all the blue and green rays of the white light, and consequently produces a red light-beam. The blue-green dress can reflect only blue and green hues. As the incident red light does not contain any such blue-green hues, the dress is unable to reflect anything at all, and therefore appears black.

II
THE MEANS OF LIGHTING

ELECTRICITY

Since all modern lighting equipment is electrical, the subject of the electric supply and installation deserves, at this stage, a brief prefatory chapter to itself, and this for two reasons.

In the first place, many photographers have little idea of the safe load-carrying capacity of their installation, and one sees cables, switches and fuses overloaded and prevented from becoming dangerous only by the fact that the whole of the lighting equipment is in use for such short periods. Secondly, the average photographer has little idea of the running costs of his lighting units until the bill comes in at the end of the quarter—when it is too late to do anything about it.

The supply company provides current at a stated voltage, and charges for it in units. Most light sources are rated in watts, with the exception of arcs, which, like switches and fuses, are rated in ampères. All these terms are inter-linked by the simplest of mathematics.

ELECTRIC UNITS

Let us draw a domestic analogy from the gas supply. The housewife when cooking the Sunday dinner frequently complains of low pressure. In order to get the dinner ready to time, she has to compensate for this low pressure by turning the taps higher and burning more cubic feet of gas.

These terms of the gas engineer have their corresponding quantities in electricity. The unit of *pressure* is the *volt*, and the unit of *current flow* the *ampère*. The equivalent of the various factors which restrict the flow of gas— the length of pipes, and notably the gas-tap—is *resistance*, measured in *ohms*. While in the gas supply the relationship between the various factors is rather complex, the relationship between the corresponding electrical terms is of the simplest.

By Ohm's law, it can be expressed alternatively as:

$$\frac{volts}{ohms} = amps. \qquad . \qquad . \qquad . \qquad . \qquad . \qquad I$$

or—

$$\frac{\text{volts}}{\text{amps}} = \text{ohms} \quad . \quad . \quad . \quad . \quad . \quad . \quad 2$$

or equally—

$$\text{amps.} \times \text{ohms} = \text{volts} \quad . \quad . \quad . \quad . \quad . \quad . \quad 3$$

Power obviously depends upon both the pressure and the amount of current. Consequently, the unit of power, the watt, is equal to the product of pressure and current:

$$\text{watts} = \text{volts} \times \text{amps.} \quad . \quad . \quad . \quad . \quad . \quad . \quad 4$$

or alternatively—

$$\text{amps.} = \frac{\text{watts}}{\text{volts}} \quad . \quad . \quad . \quad . \quad . \quad . \quad 5$$

The *unit* by which electricity is charged is based upon the watt, and is equal to a supply of 1000 watts ($=$ 1 kilowatt) for 1 hour, or any other similar multiple—for instance, 20 watts for 50 hours, 500 watts for 2 hours, or 2000 watts for $\frac{1}{2}$ hour.

It follows that to ascertain the running cost per hour of any piece of apparatus, such as a lamp, rated in watts, it is necessary only to divide the rated watts into 1000, and multiply by the cost per unit. Thus a 100-watt lamp will run for 1000/100 or 10 hours for one unit; if the cost of current is, say, 3d. per unit, then the cost is roughly one-third of a penny per hour. A 250-watt lamp will run for 1000/250 or 4 hours per unit, and, at the same price per unit, will cost $\frac{3}{4}$d. per hour.

CAPACITY OF INSTALLATION

The load-carrying capacity of any circuit or sub-circuit is always reckoned in ampères. On switches, fuses, and the company's meters one will generally find marked the permissible rating. How is one to ascertain how many lamps of given wattage can be safely run on a circuit rated at so many ampères?

The answer is to be found in equation 5. Thus, supposing it is desired to run, say, five 100-watt lamps and two 250's on a 200-v. supply, we first ascertain the total wattage, which equals 1000, and, dividing by 200, we get the answer 5 ampères.

Actually most domestic lighting circuits are rated at 5 amps., but since one would at times need to use other lights—an office light and possibly a dark-room lamp—it would be necessary in this case to have installed a 10-amp. circuit. Such a circuit could carry in addition a 500- or 750-watt electric fire; but a larger fire, of 1 KW. or more, might again lead to overloading.

FUSES

What happens when a circuit is overloaded? The cables and switches would overheat, and rapidly lead to danger, but for one safeguard: the fuses. The object of a fuse is to safeguard the rest of the installation, by blowing when the current exceeds that permissible for the installation.

D

It follows that if a fuse blows, and is replaced, and the replacement blows, the most dangerous thing to do is to put in a heavier fuse. Investigate and discover why the original fuse blew, or, if necessary, call in an electrician; never without expert advice re-wire with a heavier fuse.

Fuses are of two types. For currents up to 10 or 15 amps., ordinary wire fuses are general; if the fuse blows, it is necessary only to open the fuse-box, remove the fuse-carrier (the porcelain bar that pulls out) and insert a new piece of fuse wire *of the same gauge as before*. A distribution box in which there is a number of fuses should have each pair of fuses marked to avoid delay in replacing whichever one has blown.

Heavier fuses are generally of the cartridge type. In all installations the heaviest fuse should be near the meter, and the fuses in the distribution box, or built into the actual lamp-switch, should be lighter, so that if an accident happens and a fuse is blown, it is always the most accessible one.

Always keep at hand a card of 5-amp. fuse wire; naturally, by using it doubled the capacity of the fuse will be increased to 10 amps., so that the same wire can be used for the main fuses, unless they are of the cartridge type.

DIRECT AND ALTERNATING CURRENT

Electric supplies are of two types: *direct* and *alternating*. In the former the current flows always in the one direction—as we conveniently but erroneously say, from the positive pole to the negative. Alternating current, on the other hand, reverses its polarity many times a second. The standard frequency in England is 50 cycles, which means to say that each wire of the circuit becomes successively positive and negative 50 times every second.

Large A.C. installations are generally wired on a three-phase supply. Here we have three wires, coloured generally red, white and green, the current in each of which reverses in polarity at different instants; in addition, there may be a fourth or neutral wire, generally black. The standard voltage in this country is 230-v. single-phase or 400-v. 3-phase, either, as mentioned, 50 cycles. As we shall see later, three-phase current may be of value in connection with new types of light sources.

Strictly speaking, the five formulae previously given are applicable only to D.C. circuits, and to A.C. lighting and heating circuits. The photographer is, however, unlikely to make use of other plant, except perhaps a small fan motor, and the mysteries of *power factor* need not concern him.

RESISTANCES AND DIMMERS

A *resistance* is merely a length of wire, generally of some special alloy, mounted upon a suitable support, probably in coils, and connected in circuit with a lamp or other apparatus. So far as the photographic studio is concerned, three types of resistances may be used.

26

The most common is a variable resistance or *dimmer*, the object of which is to reduce the light intensity of a lamp (see p. 31), merely by moving a knob, which puts in circuit a varying length of wire. Another type of resistance permits of running a lamp upon a higher voltage than that for which it is made; thus in a spotlight (see p. 39), it may be preferred to use a 100-v. lamp connected through a suitable resistance to the 200-v. or 230-v. mains, in order to secure a more concentrated and better defined light spot than is possible with the higher-voltage lamp, with its larger filament. In this case the current (amps.) drawn from the mains is that indicated for the 100-v. lamp, and the surplus voltage is simply wasted as heat in the resistance; in the studio this may be undesirable, for which reason resistances are often placed away from the actual lamps.

A third type of resistance is necessary to stabilise an arc lamp (see p. 31). This type may also be adjustable, permitting the current through the arc to be varied.

CHOKES AND TRANSFORMERS

Resistances are equally suitable for A.C. or D.C. circuits. But for the former a much more efficient alternative is the *choke* for limiting current, or the *transformer* for reducing voltage. They may be identical in appearance, but differ in that the choke has only two terminals and the transformer four (or occasionally three).

A choke may be used for controlling an arc lamp, while a normal transformer will permit of running our 100-v. lamp on the higher mains voltage without the waste of current and unwanted heat of a resistance. Special types of transformers are also obtainable for running arcs, and produce a most efficient unit. Yet another type of transformer is used for stepping-up the voltage for discharge lamps.

PHOTOGRAPHIC LIGHT SOURCES

Only through constant research has science succeeded in emancipating photography from that pitiful state when freckles were a source of worry to the photographer, and a yellow flower a black indelicacy. But at the same time it must be clearly understood that colour consciousness in monochrome photography is, after all, only a question of " reproduction "; it does not give the photographer sufficient power to " create ".

It is mainly since the systematic introduction of artificial lighting into photography that the photographer has been able to disentangle himself easily from a timid objectivism, and to lift photography from the status of a purely reproductive medium. It is indeed through the artificial-light source that the photographer now has at his disposal the same mechanical flexibility as any other artist. The fact that photography of today is usually employed for purely utilitarian purposes, or that true artists seem to be still rarer in photography than in other " artistic " professions, must not be taken as proof that the photographic medium as such is still vastly inferior to other media.

Even if we would consider artificial lighting from a purely technical point of view and relate it, not to creative, but purely representational photography, the importance of the artificial-light source—in conjunction with modern negative materials—becomes at once apparent. Obviously the vast majority of the varied problems presented by advertising, commercial or even " big game " camera work could not have been solved before the photographer had the help of electricity.

But all the research put into the construction of photographic lamps is of no avail if the photographer himself does not know why all the work involved was necessary or, in other words, what is the difference between one lamp and another. We therefore have to investigate the problems of artificial-light sources and their fittings in regard to the quality and quantity of light they give out.

QUALITY AND QUANTITY OF LIGHT

The term " quality of light " refers first of all to its actinic properties. *Actinism* is the faculty of light to cause chemical changes. We call one light more actinic than another when it affects the emulsion of the negative in a higher degree. A further question of light quality is whether the light is *soft or hard, direct or indirect,* and, being direct, whether it is *spread or concentrated* (spotted).

The term " quantity of light " refers to the extent of the light-output and its bearing on the actual efficiency of the light.

Theoretically, nearly every light source can be used for the production of a photograph. In practice, we can consider as " photographic " only that lighting which has a suitable actinic quality and an intensity which enables us to take our pictures with a reasonable exposure time. (See p. 48.) We do not mean to say that we have to achieve exposures of 1/100 sec. at *f*/11 or any such " outdoor " speeds; this is not always necessary, and is even at times undesirable. But, on the other hand, our light must be efficient enough not to keep our sitter glued to his chair for so long that his expression becomes staring and his whole attitude forced and unnatural. We cannot therefore consider a light source such as a petrol lamp or a candle as " photographic lighting ", but merely as possible pictorial assets.

The reason for this becomes still more apparent when we know that a petrol flame is not only of a very limited intensity, but that the composition of its spectrum is also so exaggerated towards red that its actinic value is merely 30% for ordinary negatives, 43% for orthochromatic and approximately 60% for panchromatic materials, compared with the actinic value of a filament lamp of equal intensity.

TYPES OF LIGHT SOURCES

We can divide artificial-light sources—as used in photography—into four main groups: *tungsten filament lamps; carbon-arc lamps; discharge or vapour lamps; flash-lamps.*

Let us say right away that for the amateur, tungsten filament lighting is adequate for all general purposes where artificial lighting is to be employed; even the professional photographer seldom requires anything better. If we still consider it necessary to discuss the other three types of artificial-light sources, it is for the reason that each of them has features of its own which offer to the photographer still greater technical possibilities. It is also only by knowing *all* the material at our disposal that we can assess the true usefulness of artificial lighting and the extent to which its various peculiarities can be applied in practice.

Tungsten filament, carbon-arc, and discharge lamps can be described as " studio-lighting ". Flash-lighting, on the other hand, has a completely different application, and will not be further considered.

TUNGSTEN FILAMENT LAMPS

Tungsten filament lamps—also called incandescent filament or half-watt lamps—are hermetically sealed glass bulbs which enclose a thin wire filament.

29

This filament, acting as a resistance, becomes incandescent when electric current is transmitted through it. All modern types, which burn at a high temperature, are filled with inert gas.

The quality of the light emitted from tungsten filament lamps is different from that given out by the sun. It contains *considerably more red rays than sunlight and less blue, violet and ultra-violet rays.* Its effectiveness on ortho-chromatic materials (which are not sensitive to red) is therefore lower, its effectiveness on panchromatic emulsions higher than that of sunlight.

We have also seen that if we wish to get rid of the superfluous influence of violet-blue light-rays, we employ a yellow filter. The yellow light emitted from incandescent filament lamps acts on *orthochromatic* emulsions somewhat like a yellow filter, as the amount of the blue-violet rays contained in this kind of light is considerably reduced in comparison with sunlight.

On the other hand, the large red content of the half-watt light makes lips too bright—this applies especially when the lips have not been made up with dark-red lipstick—and blue eyes too dark when *panchromatic* negatives are used.

The spectral composition of tungsten filament light can easily be altered by " over-running " or " under-running " the bulb. This means *the higher the temperature to which the filament is heated the bluer the light, the lower the temperature of the filament the redder the light will be.* Such alterations of the spectral composition of the light not only influence the colour rendering of the negative, but also drastically change the actinic energy of the light.

For example, if we burn an electric bulb rated at 1000 watts on 200 volts with an increased energy of 240 volts (*i.e.*, an increase of 20%), we shall achieve the equivalent luminous intensity not only of a 1200-watt bulb, but also the actinic effectiveness of one of approximately 2000 watts. On the other hand, if we burn the same bulb (1000 watts) on 160 volts instead of the rated 200 volts, the actinic effectiveness produced is only equal to that produced by a 500-watt lamp.

Furthermore, the increased temperature of the filament materially increases the blue content of the light. A useful term in this connection is *colour temperature*; this term must not be confused with the actual temperature, but refers to the colour of light emitted by an incandescent object such as an arc carbon, at the absolute temperature expressed in degrees Kelvin ($0°$ K. $= -273°$ C.).

The term has a wide application; north daylight, for instance, has a colour temperature of about $6500°$ K., which is approached only by the high-intensity arc lamp. The colour temperature of a photographic filament lamp ranges from $3000°$ K. to $3500°$ K.; this is a point of practical importance only if for any reason orthochromatic emulsion is being used, since the increase in the blue-violet radiation at the higher temperature is no less than 140%.

Every electric filament, however, is constructed to work on a certain voltage; it is therefore obvious that the " *over-running* " of a lamp—i.e., *its burning at higher voltage than that stated on it*—shortens its life considerably. Now, special photographic bulbs are already over-run when working at the stated voltage, which explains why their life is much shorter than that of ordinary bulbs.

An ordinary electric bulb, as used for domestic purposes, has an expectation of life of approximately 1000 hours when being burnt on the prescribed voltage, a photographic bulb which is rated at 64 volts and burns at 110 volts has a life of only 2 hours. It is, of course, just this high over-running which makes the photo-flood bulb so very efficient, its intensity being not far less than that of an ordinary 1000-watt bulb running on its prescribed voltage. Other photographic lamps may be less over-run and their life correspondingly longer. But one should always be most careful in over-running the already over-run photographic lamps to a further extent.

For the professional photographer it is advisable to have a dimmer (see p. 26) in the studio which enables him to under-run his expensive photographic lamps during the preliminary work of posing his model or arranging a still-life composition. This under-running will make his lamps last considerably longer, and will also save money by a lower consumption of current.

The " character " of the light propagated from an incandescent filament lamp depends on the construction of the filament. *The smaller the light source—i.e., the more compact the filament—the harder is the light and the edges of the shadows cast by it.* The larger the light source—i.e., the more extended the filament—the softer is the light produced by it. It is for this reason that our domestic lamps have extended filaments of a somewhat circular construction. Projector-bulbs, burning in special reflectors or spot-light fittings, aim at a hard " effect " lighting and at well-defined shadow images; this is why they have filaments which are condensed in size so far as is practically possible.

The possibility of changing the " character " of light, by using different types of filaments, is one of the great advantages of tungsten filament lamps. Other artificial-light sources are not so flexible in this respect.

With all filament lamps, the light emission decreases as the lamp ages. When a bulb blackens it is time to discard the lamp, even though the filament may appear quite sound.

When purchasing renewals, make sure that the cap is of the right type for the fitting; lamps of under 250 watts usually have *bayonet caps*, above that size *Edison screw* or *giant screw*, while projection lamps of 1 kw. and over are preferably of the *bi-post type*.

CARBON-ARC LIGHTING

The name *carbon-arc lighting* describes very aptly its method of working. Electric current flows through two " sticks " of carbon; when these carbons touch they strike a spark in the shape of an arc, thus causing the carbons to burn off at a very high temperature.

This high temperature makes the light extremely actinic and particularly *rich in ultra-violet, violet and blue rays.* The high actinic efficiency of carbon-lighting makes it especially suitable for highlight effects. To the photographer accustomed to working with incandescents, it appears unsuitable for good colour rendering, although this failing can be overcome to a certain extent by the use of special yellow-burning carbons. A yellow filter can, of course, be used in front of the lens in order to counteract the exaggerated influx of blue and violet light-rays; but this, obviously, leads to loss of light.

The reason for these difficulties will be evident from the foregoing remarks on colour temperature. The light of the most yellow arc is still more blue than that of the incandescent lamp, since the colour temperature of an open arc burnt between plain carbons (known as *low-intensity*) is about 3550° K. When an arc is enclosed and burnt at a longer gap the light becomes more violet, and the colour temperature rises. Furthermore, *high-intensity* cored carbons, as used in film studios and occasionally in photographic studios, and also A.C. carbons, have a colour temperature ranging from 4650° K. to 6400° K.

The real merit of carbon-arc lighting is not in its intensity, but in its " character ".

The carbon-arc constitutes the most concentrated light source known to be practicable for general photographic purposes. Because of its smallness it gives off a *very hard light and produces exceedingly well-defined shadows.* It is therefore most suitable for the rendering of textures and the construction of definite shadow-patterns.   It is, on the other hand, less suitable for the lighting of " soft " forms (faces, round bowls, etc.), as the non-existence of half-tones between the areas of deep shadow and light makes modelling difficult.

Considering the particular spectral composition of carbon-arc lighting, one might assume that it would be most useful in supplementing filament-lighting, thus counteracting the latter's redundance of red. The hardness of carbon lighting, however, makes this method of colour correction inadvisable. Carbon-arc lighting should *not* be employed for " broad " lighting effects, but should be reserved for those special occasions when vigorous highlights and sharp, exact shadow-effects are to be achieved.

It is essential that an arc be burnt through a suitable resistance (see p. 26)— preferably adjustable—or from a special type of choke or reactive transformer; an ordinary lighting transformer will *not* serve.

DISCHARGE LAMPS

Discharge Lamps are glass tubes filled with a vapour which becomes luminous by means of electrical discharges. They are fundamentally different in construction from filament or carbon-arc lamps, although, like the latter, they need to be stabilised in use, generally by means of a choke. In either of the latter, light is produced by incandescence, and the spectrum is continuous; but in the discharge lamp, light is produced by what is known as resonance emission, and is concentrated into very narrow bands of the spectrum.

Two types of mercury-vapour lamps must be clearly differentiated. *The original type*, still known among older photographers as the *Cooper–Hewitt*, consists of a long tube, from 1 ft. to 6 ft. in length, sometimes bent to the form of an M. This type runs at a low gas pressure, and emits a green-blue light which is practically devoid of red rays. The *predominance of ultra-violet, violet and blue rays makes this light highly actinic, but gives at the same time a very poor colour rendering.* Red, being unable to reflect the colour of mercury-vapour light, is rendered much too dark—often even black—and the human skin takes on a ghostly appearance, the blood-vessels appearing as dark spots.

A more recent development is the *high-pressure discharge tube.* Different types are available, from an 80-watt domestic model, to a powerful 2-KW. type. In all types the light is emitted from a tiny quartz tube, 18 mm. in length and 4 mm. in diameter. The domestic types work at relatively low pressures, and produce a light not much superior to that of the older tubes; but the high-pressure lamp, working at pressures up to 100 atmospheres, produces a light having a more continuous spectrum, containing about 7% of red light, and of course very concentrated. Photographically the latter type, *except for its low emission of red rays, is comparable with the arc,* over which it has certain advantages; but, on the other hand, it needs a water supply for cooling.

Sodium-vapour lamps will be familiar to motorists, since they have been found the most satisfactory type of road-lighting. Their yellow light is also exceedingly *rich in ultra-violet and violet light-rays*, and has thus similar failings to the mercury-vapour lamp.

A point to beware of when running discharge lamps on alternating current (see p. 26)—for which all modern types are designed—is that the light fluctuates with the supply—that is to say, on a 50-cycle supply the light is extinguished 100 times a second. When making exposures of less than 1/25th second, this may cause the period during which the shutter is open to include an incomplete number of cycles, and therefore the total amount of light received will be less than the mean intensity. This difficulty can be overcome when three lamps are used, by running them on separate phases of a three-phase supply, or when two lamps are used, by feeding one through a choke and the other through a capacitor—a system which a competent electrician will understand, and which need not be further explained.

But these discharge lamps have not only disadvantages. On the contrary, they can be put to excellent use. First, their effect on panchromatic emulsions is approximately $2\frac{1}{2}$ *times more efficient than that of a tungsten filament lamp of* an equal wattage. Furthermore, low-pressure vapour-lamps—having the shape of a tube—are comparatively large-sized light sources and thus *produce a soft light.* Another advantage is that vapour-lamps *radiate considerably less heat* than filament lamps; consequently high light-intensities can be concentrated on the sitter without inconveniencing him unduly through excessive heat.

Their light is ideal in combination with incandescent filament light; this not only in order to counterbalance the red-exaggeration of the latter, but also to make the light, as such, more efficient.

E

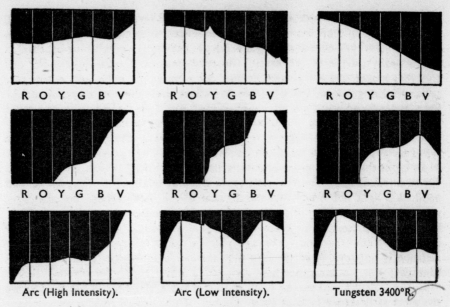

| R O Y G B V | R O Y G B V | R O Y G B V |
| R O Y G B V | R O Y G B V | R O Y G B V |

Arc (High Intensity).   Arc (Low Intensity).   Tungsten 3400°R.

Colour rendering with various light sources and on different types of films. The spectral composition of six different types of lamps is shown in the *top* rows *above* and *below*. The *centre* rows show how far orthochromatic films with their specific colour sensitivity make use of these. The *bottom* rows show how panchromatic films with their specific colour sensitivity make use of the spectral characteristics of the same lamps. (R = red, O = orange, Y = yellow, G = green, B = blue, V = violet.)

Sodium.   Mercury (Luminescent).   **Mercury.**

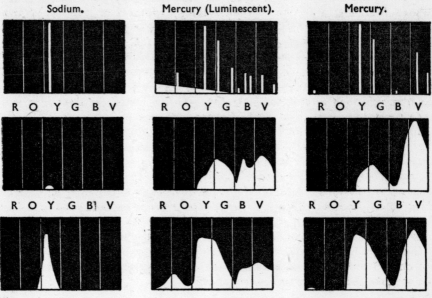

| R O Y G B V | R O Y G B V | R O Y G B V |
| R O Y G B V | R O Y G B V | R O Y G B V |

34

Low-pressure vapour-lighting is—on account of its extended source—only suitable for flood-lighting where sharp shadow-definition is not essential; it has, in this respect, characteristics exactly opposed to carbon-arc lighting. The high-pressure discharge lamp, on the contrary, is a concentrated source possessing similar properties to an arc.

Probably the most interesting future development in studio lighting will be *the low-pressure fluorescent discharge tube.* This type of source—which has already been developed for street lighting and advertising signs—consists of a low-pressure mercury tube, coated with a substance which fluoresces red or orange in the ultra-violet rays of the mercury discharge. Thus the deficiency of red in the original light is compensated for by the artificially added red, in the production of which the excess of ultra-violet is reduced. Favourable tests with such lamps have already been made in film studios.

COLOUR RENDERING WITH VARIOUS LIGHT SOURCES

The effect upon colour rendering of light of different colours is, of course, identical with that of filters of the corresponding colours, except that—with the possible exception of the sodium lamp—we rarely use light which is not at least approximately white.

Thus we should expect that with a filament lamp red would reproduce brighter than with daylight, that with a sodium lamp yellow would be brighter, and with mercury blue. (See p. 34.)

LIGHTING UNITS

It is in the nature of light to spread out from its source in all directions. The photographer has no use for this wealth of radiated energy; he must subordinate it to his purpose, must subjugate it to his intentions.

The obvious way to bar the haphazard flow of light and to guide it into one direction is to "fence" it in by means of a *reflector*. Thus, these light-rays which radiate backwards and sideways are caught and reflected into one forward stream of light.

REFLECTORS

The extent of control exercised on the direction of light depends on the construction of the reflector, but it is not sufficient merely to force light into a given channel. The photographer must also be able to control its character—that means to influence the extent of its diffusion.

We have already seen that the character of light depends largely on the size of its source; we know that the smaller the light source the harder the light, the larger the light source the softer the light produced by it. By means of adequate fittings the character of light can be still further moulded.

It now becomes apparent that light-fittings have three main tasks to perform: *Firstly* to "round up" light and to lead it into one direction; *secondly* as a consequence of its first task to intensify the light-output; *thirdly* to control the character of light.

To fulfil these various purposes two main groups of photographic fittings have been constructed: *flood-lights* and *spot-lights*.

FLOOD-LIGHTS

As the name implies, *flood-lights aim at broad effects*—at an illumination of a wide area, flooding it all over with an equal intensity. It is typical of flood-lighting that *outside its field of coverage it slowly deteriorates in luminosity, thus creating a range of half-tones which become gradually darker as they recede from the main area of illumination.*

36

A small bulb (*left*) produces less diffusion than a large bulb (*centre*). A clear glass bulb (*centre*) produces less diffusion than a frosted bulb (*right*). Both these rules apply whether the bulb is for use with or without a reflector.

A plain reflector (*left*) produces radical diffusion and directs the light very inefficiently. Conical reflectors (*centre* and *right*) direct the light better, but still give very diffused results. If the reflecting surface is smooth and polished (*centre*), there will be less diffusion than if the finish is dull and rough (*right*). This rule applies to reflectors of any shape. (In this and the other sketches, the amount of white is intended to indicate diffusion, not width of beam.)

Large reflectors (*left*) produce more diffusion than small ones (*centre*). This again applies to reflectors of any shape, not only to spherical ones as shown above. If the lamp is moved from the focal point (*right*) the amount of diffusion will again be different.

Parabolic reflectors produce less diffused, more concentrated light than spherical or conical ones. More diffusion can be obtained by shielding the bulb (*centre*) or even more by placing a diffusing screen in front of the whole reflector (*right*). This additional means of diffusion can naturally be applied to any shape of reflector.

37

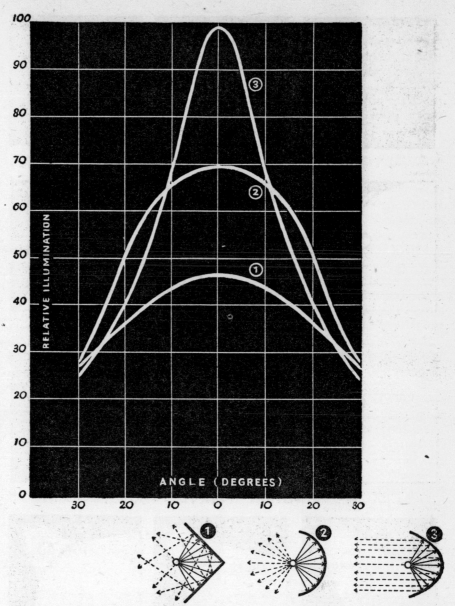

Typical curves showing the relative distribution of light produced by a conical (1), spherical (2), and parabolic (3) reflector, using the same light source. The parabolic (3) and spherical (2) reflectors compared here have both highly polished metal surfaces, while the conical reflector shown is a cardboard one. It is clearly shown that the relative illumination of the parabolic reflector (3) is the highest, but falls off rapidly towards the edges. The spherical reflector produces a more evenly distributed, softer light, but gives relatively less illumination. The conical reflector (1) leads to very diffused light and appears the least economic.

38

The shape of the reflector and the position of the lamp therein determine the extent of the area illuminated and also the quality of the light itself. *Wide, spheric, reflectors give a wider and softer beam of light, while deep, parabolic, reflectors produce a harder and more concentrated light.*

Another factor determining the character of the light is the kind of surface inside the reflector. *A dull metal finish naturally produces a more diffused light than a polished surface.* The hardest flood effects are obtained by mirror reflectors.

As already mentioned, *the position of the lamp will affect the angle of beam as well.* In the case of a parabolic mirror, moving the lamp inwards from the focal point will widen the beam; moving it forwards will narrow the beam until a point is reached where the rays cross over, when the beam commences to spread, and the efficiency falls off. In the case of a spherical mirror, any movement of the lamp from the focal point will widen the beam.

In the case of a mat reflector, the size of the reflector has a greater influence upon the softness of the beam. Obviously a *large reflector will represent a larger apparent light source than a small reflector*, and will therefore produce a more diffused illumination.

The extent of diffusion can be further controlled by the choice of bulb used, in conjunction with the reflector. *A clear glass lamp of the projector-type will give the hardest, a frosted bulb with extended filament the softest results.*

Strong diffusion is obtained by cutting off all rays directly propagated by the bulb, by fixing a " shield " in front of the bulb, thus making use of reflected light-rays only.

Still more drastic diffusion is achieved by placing a piece of thin muslin or gauze over the front of the reflector or a sheet of frosted glass between light source and object.

Flood-lighting is either produced by single units or by specially designed aggregates, these finding application on " big sets " where really wide areas have to be evenly illuminated.

Special fittings have been designed to hold a combination of filament and vapour lamps. These reflectors are usually screened by frosted glass so as to scatter the light and mix the two different kinds of light sufficiently.

Carbon-arc floods are now out of date. It has been realised that the carbon-arc light source—producing a very hard light because of its smallness—is unsuitable for flood effects; indeed, the nature of carbon lighting actually contradicts the nature of flood-lighting.

SPOT-LIGHTS

Spot-lights aim at producing a " spot " of light. This does not mean that this " spot " must necessarily be small; it is, however, implied that a *spot-light produces an accurate light—a sharply defined, spot-like area.* The cinematographer aptly designates the modern spot-light as " precision " lighting.

We have seen that flood-lighting deteriorates outside the illumination area proper—with a slow centrifugal progression. *The light-area created by spot-lighting breaks off abruptly, so that light and dark stand side by side without a wide belt of intermediary half-tones between them.* (Some types of spot-lights do produce a *small* half-tone ring around the light-periphery which, however, is so narrow that it is perceived merely as a soft edge, not as an area.)

It is thus obvious that spot-lighting is a hard light and that it produces clear-cut shadows and strong contrasts. Its purpose, therefore, is not to " flood " but to " accentuate ", not to build up a general all-round lighting but to *produce a definite pattern of light and shadow or brilliant highlight effects.*

Spot-light lamps are designed on completely different lines from flood-light lamps. While flood-lights " curb " light by capturing it by means of reflectors, spot-lights have the task of collecting and redistributing it as a beam by means of a lens which is placed in front of the light source.

By moving the light source either nearer to or farther away from the condenser lens, one is able to alter the width of the light-beam and, consequently, also the diameter of the spot of light. The nearer the light source is moved to the lens the larger will be the light-spot's diameter, the farther away the light source is from the lens the smaller will it be. (See p. 41.)

The simplest form of spot-light is that fitted with a plan-convex lens, which is flat on one side and convex on the other, the flat side facing the light source. The light-rays transmitted through this lens are refracted according to the laws of optics.

Filament spot-lights fitted with primitive condenser lenses have several faults. They not only project the lamp-filament when in focus, but they also show colour aberrations. To eliminate these faults, and also to avoid the excessive thickness of a short-focus lens (with its consequently increased risk of breakage due to heat), spot-light lenses are often used, especially in the larger sizes, in which prismatic rings appear to have been cut. What has actually been done is to step concentric areas of the lens inwards, and at the same time modify the curvature of the outer sections, producing a more even and more sharply defined spot of light.

The diameter of the spot can also be controlled by means of an iris. This is obviously inefficient from the point of view of waste of light, but on the other hand permits of producing extremely hard edges when desired.

Spot-light lamps fitted with filament bulbs produce a light of a slightly softer quality, and are therefore to be preferred to carbon-arc spots when exaggerated " hardness " seems to be out of place—as for instance in portraiture. In order to intensify the light efficiency of filament spots some makes include a mirror behind the light source.

The qualities typical of spot-lighting, *i.e., hard lighting, good definition of light and shadow edges and stringent light-control, are produced at their best by carbon-arc spot-lights.*

40

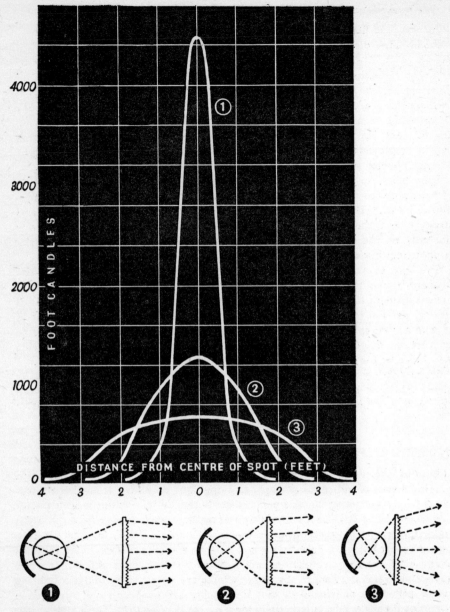

Spot-lights produce light-beams of different widths, and consequently light spots of different diameter as well as intensity, according to the relative positions of the lamp source (the lamp and the mirror behind it) and the condenser. By moving the light source farther away from the condenser (*1*) a converging light beam is produced and consequently a spot of very small diameter but of highest light intensity. The nearer the light source to the condenser lens (*2* and *3*) the wider the beam becomes, the larger the spot and the lower the light intensity.

FLOOD- AND SPOT-LIGHTS COMPARED

By means of fittings we can control the direction and the quality of light.

Flood-lights direct light into one main direction in a broad manner. The extent of the area of illumination can only be *roughly* influenced by choice of different reflectors and by the distance between the lamp and the area of illumination. It is obvious that (quite apart from the action of the light-fittings) the nearer a lamp is to a background the smaller but more luminous becomes the area of illumination. The light sources suitable for flood-lighting are filament lamps and low-pressure vapour-tubes. Flood-lighting is most usually employed for creating a general lighting on which to build up highlight effects or which serves to lighten deep shadows.

Spot-lights, on the other hand, do not merely control the general direction of light but also enable us to regulate most accurately the extent of the illuminated area. The intensity of the light weakens as the light-rays diverge, and strengthens as they converge. The size of the area of illumination here depends not only on the distance between lamp and background and the size of the lamp-fitting, but also on the focal length of the condenser lens.

The light sources employed for spot-lighting are either the carbon-arc, the filament lamp of the projector type or the high-pressure mercury lamp. When using a filament lamp, one has to watch that the broadside of the filament stands exactly parallel to the lens. Most types of projector lamps must be burnt at certain angles, specified by the manufacturer; an exaggerated tilt may, due to convection, bulge the glass. There are, however, spot-light bulbs available which can be burned at nearly every angle.

Flood-lighting as well as spot-lighting can be diffused (softened) at will by either fabric or glass "diffusers". Leaving this fact out of account, we can classify light sources and fittings in their "light-quality" as shown on p. 37.

INDIRECT LIGHTING

Besides the light sources already discussed, the photographer can also employ means of indirect lighting, *i.e.*, using light only after it has been intercepted by a reflective surface and redistributed by it. When working with artificial lighting it is best to employ *mat white cardboards as reflectors*. (It is unfortunate that in common usage the term "reflector" is used to describe two different things, a light-fitting and a light-reflecting surface.) As we have seen (see p. 19), these reflect up to 80% of the incident light and produce at the same time very soft tones. Stronger effects are obtained by indirect lighting when reflectors consisting of *mat silver-paper* are used and we can achieve vigorous highlight effects by employing a *mirror* as reflector. *Shiny silver-paper* reflectors are not to be recommended, as they produce scattered and irregular reflections which are difficult to control. Indirect light sources are invaluable for the rendering of purely reflective objects, like silver, etc.

42

A factor that must not be overlooked when we are striving for low-key or contrasty effects is the reflection and diffusion of light due to the walls of the room. In a large studio this may be relatively unimportant, but *in a small room with light walls, the repeated reflections may make it impossible to secure dark shadows.*

To overcome such difficulties, the cine-cameraman makes use of sheets of black material, which he descriptively calls *niggers*, and which he uses to shield any unwanted light—either stray light from a lamp or reflections from the set—from his shadow areas.

Similarly, small screens of lightproof or slightly translucent material cut out to circular or other curved shapes can be fixed on a swivelling rod attached to a standard to cut off areas of direct or reflected light and create small fields of shadow on the subject.

LIGHTING OUTFIT FOR STUDIO AND HOME

Let us now try to form some idea as to the kind and the number of light-fittings required by amateur and professional photographers in consideration of the various tasks they might wish to perform.

The size of a light-fitting depends primarily on the size of the light source; the size of the light source depends on the power of its light-output. Generally speaking the higher the wattage of a bulb the larger the reflector required. Thus, the choice of light-fittings must be subordinated to the individual photographer's practical requirements.

The amateur, therefore, working at home tackling only small " sets " and not aiming at the highest possible shutter speeds, will not inconvenience himself with the large and expensive professional fittings.

The professional photographer, on the other hand, must carefully consider the number and kinds of lamps he is going to buy. It is obvious that he will also have to consider his purse, but the decisive factor for his choice is governed by his requirements. It will not do to try to save money by buying a few small fittings and then attempt to tackle pictorial problems which can only be solved by an expensive and efficient lighting equipment.

For the *amateur with humble intentions* three reflectors fitted with photographic bulbs are adequate. They serve the purpose of taking the wife and the kiddies.

The *ambitious amateur* who wants to try his hand on proper portrait-studies or still-life pictures should acquire a more professional outfit. One small spot-light fitted with a 500-watt projector lamp and two or three flood-reflectors fitted with 250- or 500-watt filament lamps are recommended.

To determine the *professional* photographer's needs in regard to lighting equipment is not so easy. Keeping in mind that we have two different aspects to take into account, the photographer's scope and his method of working, and that we have to allow for slight adjustments because of personal prefer-

43

ences, I believe that the following suggestions will give quite a good idea of what is necessary as a minimum.

LIGHTING EQUIPMENT FOR THE PORTRAIT PHOTOGRAPHER.

1 mercury-vapour and filament-lamp combination flood-unit.
2–4 500-watt floods.
2 1000-watt (1-KW.) filament spot-lights.
Diffusers and paper reflectors.

Consumption: on 230-v., A.C. only: 4 to 5 KW. (18 to 25 amps.).

LIGHTING EQUIPMENT FOR THE ADVERTISING-PHOTOGRAPHER SPECIALISING IN STILL-LIFE.

2 500-watt floods.
1 1000-watt flood.
1 250-watt flood.
1 carbon-arc spot-light (approx. 25 amps.).

Consumption: on 100/110-v. D.C. or A.C., with arc resistance: 5 KW. (50 amps.); on 200/230-v. D.C. or A.C., with arc resistance: 7 to 8 KW. (30 to 40 amps.); on 230-v. A.C., with reactive transformer for arc: 3½ KW. (15 amps.).

LIGHTING EQUIPMENT FOR THE ADVERTISING-PHOTOGRAPHER.

2 500-watt floods in spheric reflectors.
2 flood aggregates, each consisting of four 500-watt lamps.
1 2-KW. flood-projector-type bulb in large reflector which produces a hard light.
2 2-KW. filament spot-lights.
1 1-KW. " overhead " spot-light.
1 carbon-arc spot-light.

Consumption: on 100/110-v. D.C. or A.C., with arc resistance: 15 KW. (150 amps.); on 200/230-v. D.C. or A.C., with arc resistance: 17 to 18 KW. (75 to 90 amps.); on 230-v. A.C., with reactive transformer for arc: 13½ KW. (60 amps.).

LIGHTING EQUIPMENT FOR THE FASHION PHOTOGRAPHER.

2 500-watt floods.
2 flood aggregates, each consisting of four 500-watt lamps.
1 flood aggregate to be operated from ceiling; at least 4000-watt.
1 " overhead " spot-light preferably carbon arc.
1 carbon-arc spot-light.
2–3 incandescent-filament spot-lights of 2000 watts each.
1 background projector.

Consumption: on 100/110-v. D.C. or A.C., with arc resistance: 20 to 24 KW. (180 to 240 amps.); on 200/230-v. D.C. or A.C., with arc resistances: 25 to 35 KW. (110 to 175 amps.); on 230-v. A.C., with reactive transformers for arcs: 17 to 20 KW. (75 to 90 amps.).

The foregoing figures for current consumption are based upon the whole of the equipment being in use at one time. In practice this would, in the case of the third and fourth suggestions, probably never be necessary, and a lighter installation would in most cases be adequate.

EQUIPPING A STUDIO

If you are equipping a studio for the first time you must realise that the choice of the right kind of lighting equipment is of the utmost importance. Before buying lighting equipment, make up your mind which branch of photography you are going to specialise in.

44

Not only this. Ask yourself if you are sure that you have found a definite " style " of working. If you have not, it is better to buy, at first, the absolute minimum you need just to carry on, and to supplement your equipment as experience makes you aware of your needs. If, on the other hand, you have a style of your own let this govern your choice.

The photographer who aims at hard and contrasty effects and prominent shadow pattern will rely to a far greater extent on spot-lighting than the photographer who works in soft flat tones relieved only by a few accentuating highlights.

LAMP-STANDS AND FIXTURES

It is not for us to describe all kinds of lamp-stands and fixtures on the market. The manufacturers' catalogues give ample information about the various types available. At the same time it seems necessary to discuss this matter from the point of view of the practising photographer—amateur or professional.

It is obvious that the construction of a lamp-stand depends to a great extent on the size and weight of the lamp it has to carry. The amateur does not require any heavy and elaborate " tripods ", which would only be a nuisance to him. There are a few rather complicated-looking lamp aggregates available, e.g., stands holding three flood reflectors, each of which can be moved separately and in every conceivable angle. This lamp-stand looks most efficient at a first glance, but I still consider three separate lamps to be more efficient than the more expensive aggregate.

The importance of keeping our lamp equipment flexible is repeatedly stressed in this book. The amateur especially, who does not require a huge bank of light for general flood effects, is not justified in hampering his freedom of action by unnecessarily complicated fixtures.

For the professional photographer these problems are not so easily solved. Not only has he heavy lamps requiring a sturdy support, but he may also need a light-source which covers a very wide field of illumination. We have to distinguish between two groups of lamp supports—stands and wall or ceiling fixtures.

Lamp-stands should run on large castors and be easily movable; this applies especially when the stand carries a heavy lamp. Another point to be watched is that the lamp can be *elevated to a good height* without *undue effort* and again that it can be *lowered almost to the ground.*

The average portrait or advertising photographer should restrict himself to separate lamps whenever possible. Studios are too often overloaded with gadgets on ceilings and walls, which—although extremely impressive—prove in practice to be more of a hindrance than a help to creative work. It is only by moving all his lamps wherever he may want them that the photographer can make full use of the many technical and creative possibilities of artificial lighting. Fixed light sources have not only a restricted radius of action; they also

45

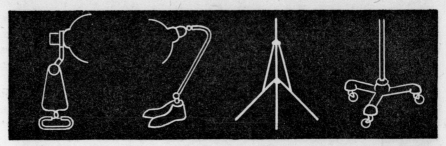

Examples of lamp bases. *From left to right:* (*1*) Clamp-on unit allows secure attachment to any vertical or horizontal support. (*2*) Table lamps can be placed on any flat surface and are useful in locations where floor space is limited. (*3*) Tripods are mostly used in connection with light telescopic stands. (*4*) The studio base with ball-bearing casters provides the most convenient and most rigid means of positioning.

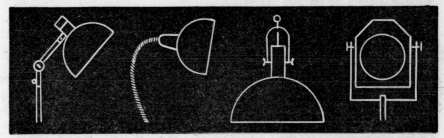

Methods of lamp adjustment. (*1*) May be clamped at any angle. (*2*) Provides added flexibility, but is apt to lose its rigidity. (*3*) and (*4*) are usual methods of supporting spot-lights and other heavy fittings.

Methods of adjusting light sources. (*1*) Provides vertical and angular adjustment. (*2*) Provides lateral adjustment. In (*3*) the light sources can be adjusted in a variety of positions. If close together a harder light will be produced than if they are separated. (*4*) is a universal fitting providing adjustment of the lamp over a large area

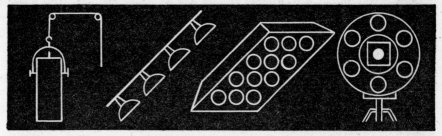

(*1*), (*2*) and (*3*) are three different types of overhead fittings, giving progressively a softer illumination. In (*1*) the lamp is masked to cover a small area and can be adjusted for height or angle. (*4*) is a fitting for shadowless lighting, the lamps in a ring reflector surrounding the camera.

46

induce the photographer to base his ideas on the limited scope of " ready for use " and more or less stable conditions of lighting. It is in this way that imagination becomes sterile and static.

However—let us not generalise, for there are occasions when fixtures are needed. *Studios specialising in photographing of big sets*, groups and elaborate fashion arrangements might be unable to produce the necessary *all-round illumination* without some kind of light source which illuminates the set from a good distance and from a good height. It is for these requirements that *bank-lighting* has been constructed which moves freely along the ceiling by means of steel runners.

Another fixture universally useful is the *overhead spot- or flood-lamp*. In order to achieve direct top lighting, it is obviously necessary to suspend the lamp from the ceiling.

Whatever our requirements, whatever our personal inclinations, we should always remember that we must not be bluffed by looks when buying our lamp-stands. A small collapsible flood-tripod, recommendable to the amateur, might often be more practicable than a heavy chromium-plated affair which serves the same purpose. One is too easily tempted to leave many possibilities untried, just because the inconvenience of moving heavy lamps makes the execution of an idea appear far more difficult than it is in reality.

THE ESTIMATION OF EXPOSURE

The whole object of photographic lighting is to produce on the negative an exposure which, when printed through to a positive, will reproduce the light and shade of the original subject, not necessarily as they actually existed, but as the aesthetic taste of the photographer dictates.

Exposure is possibly the most controversial subject in the whole realm of photography. To a certain extent one can reduce it to scientific terms—to the reproduction within a given tone range on the negative of the range of light intensities of the subject. But innumerable factors, aesthetic and practical (the latter including the developing of the negative and the making of the print) suggest that any such method can certainly never provide a final dictum.

BRIGHTNESS RANGE AND DEVELOPMENT

Let us dispel once and for all the illusion that incorrect exposure can always be compensated for in development. Certainly, if we have an under-exposed plate, as development proceeds the highlights will gradually increase in contrast; but the shadows will still be clogged. Similarly, if the plate is over-exposed, it may be possible by a very brief development to prevent the highlights burning out, but we shall hardly be able to obtain a satisfactory print. However, the photographer's classic rule that *over-exposure is better than under-exposure* contains a considerable measure of truth.

The greater the brightness range of a subject, the more accurate must be the exposure. If we have a subject with a small brightness range, the exposure may vary over a range of as much as 10 to 1, and we shall still get a negative which, given suitable development, will produce a satisfactory print, with both highlight and shadow detail. But if on the other hand we have a subject with a much wider brightness range, the exposure must be precise, and the negative must be developed to give a soft negative all the tones of which can be printed through to the positive.

It will be apparent that when we refer to subject brightness we *do not mean the visual brightness, but the brightness as seen by the photographic emulsion.*

48

Thus to an orthochromatic emulsion a pure red, no matter how brightly lit, could never be over-exposed (although let it be emphasised that few reds, or any other colours, are actually pure!).

It is, however, assumed that for all work with artificial light, panchromatic materials will be used and visual brightness is therefore a fairly safe guide, an exception being when filters are used.

FACTORS DETERMINING EXPOSURE

A number of factors having a direct bearing on the subject of exposure have already been briefly mentioned. Ignoring for the moment aesthetic considerations, let us list these and other practical factors under three headings: those attributable to the subject, those inherent in the negative material and those forming part of subsequent treatment. In each horizontal section are included co-acting factors.

Subject.	Negative Material.	Subsequent Treatment.
Intensity of Light Brightness of Subject	Speed of Emulsion	Degree of Development
Colour of Light Colour of Subject Colour of Filters	Colour Sensitivity of Emulsion	
Brightness Range of Subject	Latitude of Emulsion	Accuracy of Development

This table takes no account of the vital factor of *lens aperture*, as—apart from the effect upon the depth of focus—its influence can be stated precisely.

DETERMINATION OF EXPOSURE

Notwithstanding all these complications, one customarily sees the professional portrait photographer just take the cap off his lens and give what appears to be quite an arbitrary exposure. But, apart from the possibility that the exposure is less arbitrary than it appears, he is safeguarded by two important facts: that the brightness range of his subject is rarely very wide; and that he may even prefer the shadows to be a little clogged in order to produce a bolder print. If he should be seriously at fault, he is still saved by the fact that his plates are developed individually, and can be taken out of the developer at the moment when experience indicates that shadow detail has appeared.

Modern photography, however, increasingly demands a full use of the permissible tone range. Furthermore, modern processing methods generally do not permit of individual attention being given to every one of a large number of negatives; the amateur who patronises the local chemist is especially liable to find that, in the effort to compensate for the usual run of under-exposed snapshots, a negative that is in the least over-exposed may be developed to a state where the highlights are hopelessly clogged.

G

How are we to eliminate guesswork (or, as the photographer no doubt prefers to call it, experience) and replace it by some precise method of exposure determination?

Innumerable exposure tables have been prepared, which give exposure factors for a varying number of lamps of various wattages, at different distances from the subject, for different lens stops and for various emulsion speeds; by adding these factors together, one is able to consult a table in which the exposure time is found opposite the total of the factors.

How it is possible for these tables to allow for such factors as the differences in the angular positioning of lamps, for the innumerable types of reflectors used with varying degrees of light efficiency, for varying subject brightness, and for such trivial happenings as variations in line volts, a blackened lamp, or a dusty reflector, is obscure. To take one of these factors alone, the light emission of a filament lamp varies as the *fifth* power of the line volts! The value of such tables is demonstrated by a recently published statement that the proportion of successful negatives obtained by them is under 50%.

EXPOSURE NOMOGRAM

However, a chapter on exposure would be obviously incomplete without some guidance of this nature. While it cannot be claimed that the nomogram reproduced is greatly superior to the average exposure table in regard to the prime quantities, it has been specially calculated to permit at least of a rather closer mathematical approximation of the final result.

To use it, find along line 1 the point corresponding to the type of lamp and reflector used. In line 2 find the distance of the lamp from the subject; draw a line between these points in lines 1 and 2 and extend it to cut the line 3. In line 4 find the speed of the emulsion, and join lines 3 and 4, cutting the line 5. In line 6 find the lens aperture it is proposed to use, and join the point in line 5 with this point. The point at which the line 7 is cut will indicate the exposure time in seconds. Thus by merely drawing three lines, all the essential factors of exposure can be at least approximately taken into account.

Where more than one lamp is used, deal with the first lamp as described, but note the number found on line 3. Then deal similarly with the other lamps, and add together the numbers so found, using this total on line 3 to connect up with line 4.

This nomogram relates to subjects of medium brightness, e.g., average portraits. For light subjects (e.g., a blonde sitter dressed in white clothes, or light-coloured objects generally) decrease exposure by $\frac{1}{2}$ to $\frac{2}{3}$ (1 or $1\frac{1}{2}$ lens stops). For dark subjects (e.g., dark materials, dark unpolished furniture) increase exposure by two or three times (1 or $1\frac{1}{2}$ lens stops larger).

For the benefit of the mathematically minded, this nomogram is a graphical solution of the equation:

$$E = \frac{f^2 K}{I \cdot S} = \frac{f^2 K}{S\left(\dfrac{L_1 e_1}{D_1^2} + \dfrac{L_2 e_2}{D_2^2} + \cdots\right)}$$

where:

E = exposure in seconds.
f = lens aperture.
K = a constant.
I = incident light (foot-candles).
S = speed of emulsion (H. & D.).
L = emission of lamp.
e = efficiency of reflector.
D = distance of lamp from subject.

50

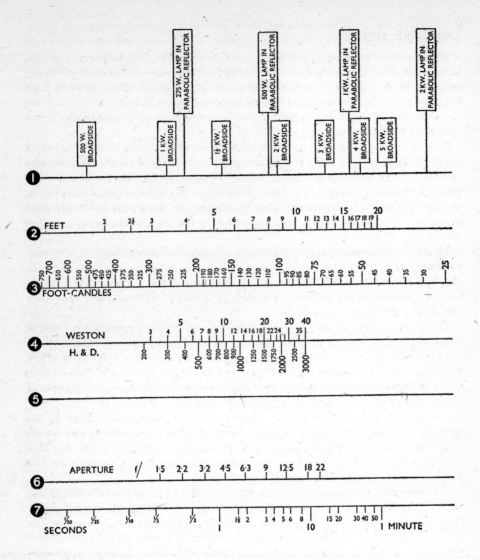

1

| 500 W. BROADSIDE | 1 KW. BROADSIDE | 275 W. LAMP IN PARABOLIC REFLECTOR | 1½ KW. BROADSIDE | 500 W. LAMP IN PARABOLIC REFLECTOR | 2 KW. BROADSIDE | 3 KW. BROADSIDE | 1 KW. LAMP IN PARABOLIC REFLECTOR | 4 KW. BROADSIDE | 5 KW. BROADSIDE | 2 KW. LAMP IN PARABOLIC REFLECTOR |

2 FEET   2   2½   3   4   5   6   7   8   9   10   11 12 13 14   15 16 17 18 19   20

3 FOOT-CANDLES   750 700 650 600 550 500 475 450 425 400 375 350 325 300 275 250 225 200 190 180 170 160 150 140 130 120 110 100 95 90 85 80 75 70 65 60 55 50 45 40 35 30 25

4 WESTON   3   4   5   6 7 8 9   10   12 14 16 18   20   22 24   30 40   35
H. & D.   200   300   400   500   600 700 800 900 1000   1250   1500 1750 2000   2500   3000

5

6 APERTURE   f/   1·5   2·2   3·2   4·5   6·3   9   12·5   18 22

7   1/50   1/25   1/10   1/5   1/2   1   1½ 2   3 4 5 6 8   10   15 20   30 40 50   1 MINUTE
SECONDS

Exposure nomogram. Find along line *1* the type of lamp and unit used. In line *2* find the distance of the lamp from the subject; draw a line from these points in lines *1* and *2*, cutting the line *3*. In line *4* find the speed of the emulsion, and join lines *3* and *4*, cutting the line *5*. In line *6* find the lens aperture, and join the point in line *5* with this point. The point at which the line *7* is cut will indicate the exposure time in seconds. This exposure nomogram suggests very generous exposure times, in preference to errors on the under-exposure side

51

EXPOSURE METERS

Obviously a far more satisfactory method than the calculation of light intensities is to measure them. Experience with the various types of exposure meters shows that, in contrast to the use of exposure tables, a very high proportion of successful results can be obtained by their use.

Two types of exposure meters are in common use, respectively the *visual type* and the *photo-electric type*.

The former consists of some form of *optical wedge*—a strip or more usually a circle of glass, varying from almost complete transparency to almost complete opacity, either continuously or in steps. In some types, the scene is viewed through the wedge, which is rotated until either the shadow detail disappears, or the highlights only are just visible; in other types, the wedge is rotated until a number inside the meter, corresponding to the step of the wedge, is just visible.

Photo-electric meters are, of course, the simplest to manipulate; it is merely necessary to point the instrument towards the scene (or in some cases towards the lights) and read off the required exposure from a scale. Most types embody slide-rules for adjusting the exposure to suit different lens apertures and different emulsion speeds.

On average subjects with average lighting, any of these meters are capable of excellent and reliable results. But for certain out-of-the-ordinary subjects —to be more precise, subjects embodying an unusually wide brightness range with particularly unequal areas of highlight and shadow—two of these three types are open to a *serious defect: that they merely integrate the over-all brightness of the scene, and take no account of the brightness range*, or of the fact that it may be just a small area of highlight or shadow that is the centre of interest of the picture, and must therefore be exposed for. The exception is the visual extinction meter, in which the scene is viewed through the wedge; for this reason, this meter is to be recommended on any occasion where accuracy and selectivity are preferred to ease of manipulation.

Consider two successive photographs, in which the same model wearing the same clothes and with the same lighting is posed, first before a light background, then before a dark one. Any type of integrating meter would give widely differing exposures for these two pictures, which in reality would need almost identical exposures. In such a case, the meter should be directed upon that part of the scene for which it is desired to expose; a photo-electric meter can be so used, but with a visual meter matters are simplified.

For normal subjects, the visual extinction meter can be used in the manner recommended by the manufacturers—that is to say, upon either the shadows or highlights, according to the method of calibration. The former is perhaps preferable, since generally one prefers to ensure shadow detail at the risk of burnt-out highlights.

But where a subject has a long brightness range, it is quite feasible to *make*

52

two readings, one on the shadows and the other on the highlights; a few tests with the individual meter will be necessary to discover what range of readings is permissible to fall within the exposure range of the emulsion, but once these tests are made, it is a simple matter to make a correction of one reading by the second, or alternatively to reflect a little more light towards the shadows.

A type of instrument possessing certain advantages over the ordinary exposure meter is the *G.E.C. Visual Photometer,* in which, by matching the brightness of a part of the subject with that of an illuminated wedge, the intensity in foot-candles (or in the present case, foot-lamberts) can be ascertained. This instrument may be used in conjunction with the nomogram on p. 51, since the calibrations of line 3 are in foot-candles.

In any case, the meter should be used from as close as possible to the camera position, to allow for the possibility of any specular reflections shining into the lens. The condition of the eyes naturally affects the reading; never try to use the meter after you have been looking at the lights, nor on the other hand when you have just emerged from the dark-room.

FILTER FACTORS

Almost invariably *the use of a filter involves an increase in exposure* (see p. 15). The amount of increase due to a particular filter is known as the filter factor.

One commonly speaks of a three-times filter or a five-times filter, indicating usually yellow filters needing three or five times the normal exposure. But actually it is impossible to consider filter factor without reference both to the light source and to the emulsion.

Consider the case of a red filter. Used with panchromatic stock in daylight, it will cut the ultra-violet, blue, and green bands—three-quarters of the total available light—and will consequently need about a four-times increase in exposure. On the other hand, used with an orthochromatic stock, it will cut practically all the usable light rays, and will increase the exposure enormously.

Again, using the same filter with incandescent lighting, it will not cut as much as three-quarters of the light, because such light sources are richer in red emission. Consequently, using panchromatic emulsion, the filter factor may be only about 2. With sodium lighting the filter will probably cut none at all of the light, and the factor will be 1; with mercury lighting it will on the other hand cut probably 90% or more of the light, and the factor will be from 10 to 15.

A filter factor is therefore entirely meaningless unless it is specified as correct for the stock and the illuminant actually used. By comparing the transmission spectrogram of the filter with the sensitivity spectrogram of the emulsion, and bearing in mind the characteristics of the lighting, it is, however, possible to assess the factor with some degree of accuracy, although experiment is of course the safest way.

III

THE PRINCIPLES OF LIGHTING

BUILDING UP THE LIGHTING

There is only one way of learning how to build up photographic lighting—by learning to " see ". There is also only one way of learning how to apply this photographic lighting—by learning to feel sensitively and to think intelligently.

Rules *are* essential to guide the student and to acquaint him with the wealth of experiences accumulated by masters of his profession. However, let us once and for all realise that photographic lighting can never be taught *or* learnt by hard-and-fast rules alone.

But one thing the student *can* be taught, namely, how to use light and shadow in order to perform the task which he *himself* has set.

THE DIRECTION OF LIGHT

The direction of light determines the form of an object. The term " direction of light " describes *the relation of the line of light-incidence to the line of camera-vision. The smaller the angle between these two lines—i.e., the more they coincide—the flatter appears the image. The more the angle between these two lines widens towards 90°, the more contrast is created.* As the angle widens towards 180°, the shadow element becomes more predominant until the area of light is ultimately confined to a very narrow rim. (See pp. 58–59.)

It is difficult to give rules, but we can safely say that the best form-rendering of a three-dimensional object is achieved by a light which meets the line of camera-vision at an angle between 45° and 90°. The exact position at which a lamp should be placed in order to give the ideal form rendering cannot be theoretically determined, as it varies according to the form of the object.

The need for intelligent planning becomes all the more stressed by the fact that the direction of light is also instrumental in forming the character of the picture. We shall see later how the existence of shadow helps to create a dramatic effect and that the dramatic impression becomes more emphasised as the shadow element of the picture becomes more pronounced. In other words: *the larger the angle between the line of light-incidence and the line of camera-vision, the more " dramatic " is the pictorial effect.*

One would assume that every photographer, appreciating the great import-

56

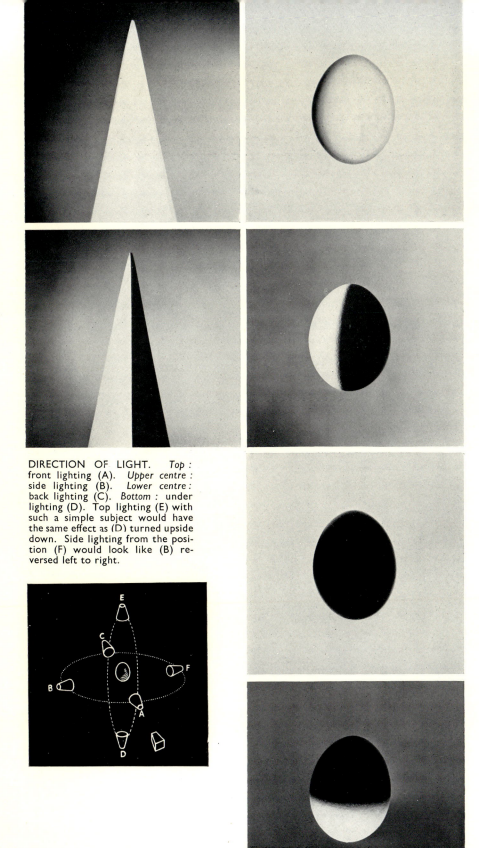

DIRECTION OF LIGHT. *Top :* front lighting (A). *Upper centre :* side lighting (B). *Lower centre :* back lighting (C). *Bottom :* under lighting (D). Top lighting (E) with such a simple subject would have the same effect as (D) turned upside down. Side lighting from the position (F) would look like (B) reversed left to right.

DIRECTION OF LIGHT. *Upper row :* the effect of moving the light from the position of acute side light (A) to almost back light (F). *Upper centre row :* the effect of moving the light upwards from the position (G) to (K), the latter being acute top lighting. *Lower centre row :* the effect of moving the light diagonally from the position (L) to (N). *Bottom left :* under lighting (O). *Bottom right :* dead front lighting (P).

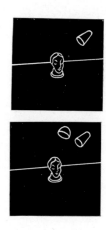

BUILDING UP THE LIGHTING.
Top : spot light serves as basic
light. *Upper centre :* a flood has
been added as a supplementary to
soften the shadows. *Lower centre:*
a bank of floods has been introduced
in front of the subject to give
general illumination. *Bottom :*
special lighting for the background
brings relief and the finishing touch.

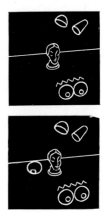

ance of the direction of light, preconsiders the placing of his lamps most carefully. Unfortunately there are only too many who prefer a " safe " lighting (*i.e.*, a flat, shallow and senseless flooding of the object which avoids " dangerous " shadows) to the more strenuous occupation of logical thinking and experiment. I advise the student most strongly to spare no effort to learn how an object (it may be a face, a flower-bowl or a match-box) alters its appearance under the varying angles of light incidence. These experiments are very easily executed. All one needs is a single lamp which is to be moved slowly around the object, and the patience necessary to study and note the varying changes effected in this way. (See pp. 58–59.)

TERMS

The photographer has terms which he needs for describing certain kinds of lighting. These terms are based on the position of the light source in its relation to the object. (See p. 57.)

We start with *front-lighting*, *i.e.*, a light produced by a light source placed right in front of the object. If we now move the light source *horizontally* we obtain *side-lighting*, and when continuing this movement *rim-lighting* and, finally, *back-lighting*.

If we move the light source *vertically* (again starting from a front position) we will obtain *top-lighting* or *under-lighting* respectively and when carried far enough again rim- or back-lighting.

Moving the lamp *diagonally upwards*, we obtain *cross-lighting* which is, as we shall see later, most useful in portraiture and figure photography.

THE FIRST STEP: VISUALISING

Before you move a single lamp—indeed, before you even decide what lighting to employ for the making of a picture—make up your mind what you want to do. Visualise composition and pictorial balance after knowing what you wish your picture to express.

Before deciding on the particular lighting technique to be employed for your pictorial problem, you must *feel* the " atmosphere " you want to convey. A rough rule to remember is, that *pictures full of shadow or darkness* (low-key pictures) *have a greater tendency to create emotional effects than those lighting compositions which consist predominantly of light and subtle middle tones* (high-key pictures).

Only after having planned the atmosphere you want to breathe into the pictorial framework can you select the kind of lighting and, consequently, the kind of lamps you are going to use. If we look back (see p. 37) we shall find that the different kinds of light sources and the special diffusers used in combination with various negative materials give us a complete control.

Allowing for exceptions to the rule, we can safely assume that *soft effects*

H 2   61 find their applications mostly in " high-key " pictures, while " low-key " treatment depends more on hard contrasts and " bite." Generally, subjects with a masculine flair require a bold and vigorous approach, while pictures featuring the feminine element usually " cry " for softness, half-tones and glamour.

THE SECOND STEP: THE BASIC LIGHT

Every lighting scheme must be built up *logically*. Artificial lighting as employed for photography should not be the outcome of a haphazard playing about, for we can only build up lighting according to our intentions if we develop it by a systematic method of working progressively step by step. It will not do to switch on all the lamps at once, shifting them here and there and hoping for the best.

Make it a habit to shut out all daylight or unwanted artificial light before starting with the building up of the lighting. When working with artificial lighting it is essential that you have every effect and all the tone-values of your composition strictly under control; this is, however, only possible if any incidental stray-lighting is eliminated.

Start your lighting with one lamp only: the basic light. This light is not called " basic " merely because it constitutes the first practical step, but because it is the light which must in itself demonstrate the intentions of the photographer in a rough manner; it must therefore also govern all subsequent lighting developments.

It has to be realised that the term " basic light " does not refer to any special kind of light. Here are a few examples.

If we wish to treat the subject as a silhouette or half-silhouette, the basic light will obviously be a light illuminating the background. In a pure silhouette (p. 91) this basic light will constitute the total amount of lighting needed in the picture.

In the semi-silhouette (p. 92) the basic light is again the lighting on the background, but it is supplemented by a more or less diffused light on the subject. The supplementary light serves to lighten the subject and to bring it into the right relationship with the luminosity of the background.

On the other hand, if we wish to photograph a profile portrait and emphasise the facial characteristics by a vigorous rim of light (p. 92) along its contours, the basic light will be the rim light. The tone of the background and the further light effects on the face will have to be regarded as of secondary importance.

THE THIRD STEP: THE SUPPLEMENTARY LIGHT

While the basic light is mostly produced by one lamp only, the secondary or supplementary light can be created by any number of lamps. The purpose of every supplementary light is to bring the idea roughly indicated by the basic light to pictorial completeness. *In no circumstances should the supplementary*

62

light contradict the meaning of the basic light, but always emphasise its significance.

If we again take the example of a face in profile which is basically lit by a rim of light along its outline, the supplementary lights employed in such a picture would be:—

First Supplementary Light: on background if we wish to have a background other than black.

Second Supplementary Light: a general flood on the face to bring the completely black parts of the face up to a standard of luminosity which conforms with our intention.

Third Supplementary Light: Spot-light effect from behind the sitter so as to produce a new rim light along the back of the sitter's head, at the same time lighting up the hair.

I want to mention at this stage that *if the object is detached from the background, object (foreground unit) and background should be lighted as separate units,* even when they form one entity in composition. Only thus is it possible to control the tone values on the background.

THE LAST STEP: BACKGROUND PROJECTION

The name implies that, firstly, light and shadow as produced by this method are used solely on the background; secondly, that the pattern itself is created by means of projection. By means of background projection one can obtain two distinctly different effects.

An abstract background pattern which has no other purpose than to fill in empty background space. This kind of background projection can in certain circumstances be most helpful in building up a composition and in leading the eye towards the main unit of the picture.

A realistic background unit such as a landscape or any other kind of scenery. This second application of background projection is used to make studio photographs look like outdoor shots. It ought to be noted that even if one succeeds in bringing the foreground unit into the right perspective with the projected background, these efforts are only seldom successful. It is for this reason that this second kind of background projection is rarely used for really good photographic illustrations but mainly for cheap catalogue work.

Background projection is achieved by specially constructed projectors of a spot-light type fitted with an incandescent filament lamp. Geometrical patterns are cast by cut masks (metal or cardboard) which are inserted into the projector between the light source and lens, while realistic images are projected by means of lantern slides.

A background on which an image has been projected must not be touched by any other light. Even the smallest amount of stray lighting can weaken the projected image to such an extent that it becomes insignificant and without purpose.

63

It is advisable to use background projection as sparingly as possible and to try to make pictures without this often misunderstood and over-rated photographic method.

DAYLIGHT

It is nowadays only seldom that one finds a professional photographer who habitually mixes daylight and studio light. To him this combination does not offer any advantages which would compensate for the loss of reliability incurred by the ever-changing conditions of daylight.

For the amateur, however, this combination is still of great importance. Most amateurs have only a limited number of lamps at their disposal, and they seldom possess a spot-light by which they can obtain the brilliant highlights and well-defined shadow forms of direct sunlight.

The method to be employed in building up the lighting is here exactly the same as when working with artificial lighting. Again we have to start with one light source only—namely, with the one creating the *basic* light. When employing direct sunlight we shall use this as the basic light source and treat it like a spot-light. We shall then use our (weaker) artificial-light sources—or reflector—for the secondary effects, such as shadow dilution or supplementary highlights.

If we have only diffused daylight at our disposal, we shall produce our basic light with the artificial-light source and use the daylight as " flood ".

I do not recommend the use of combined artificial lighting and daylight for *still-life* photography because of the inflexibility of the daylight source. Especially when dealing with small objects this shortcoming becomes clearly apparent. For portrait studies, on the other hand, this kind of light combination can be employed to great advantage, and one must not limit one's experiments to purely " straight shots ". Even big close-ups and angle shots can be most effectively handled in this way. Here, as everywhere else, the result depends to a far greater extent on the talent and skill of the photographer than on his equipment. Indeed, one photo-flood bulb in a reflector, one sheet of white paper and a window is an absolutely sufficient and excellent equipment for a wide range of photographic possibilities.

PRIMITIVE LIGHT SOURCES

Primitive light sources, such as a match, candle or oil lamp, etc., are not to be assessed as tools for creating a photographic image, but merely as " props " serving to enhance the pictorial effect or to tell a story.

This statement does not imply that there are no circumstances when a primitive light source can be used successfully in the making of a photograph; but the occasions when a candle or a camp fire constitutes the only source of photographic lighting are rare. The primitive light source does not freely adapt itself to the intentions of the photographer; anyway, it would be futile to use light sources of inadequate intensity when even the amateur has cheap and efficient photographic lamps at his disposal.

Another point not to be overlooked is that although a situation might appear to our eye as picturesque in the romantic light of a coal fire or the halo of an oil lamp, it does not necessarily follow that it will be registered just as attractively by the camera; in fact, we shall often find when examining our negative that contrasts have been exaggerated and a great amount of " atmosphere " lost.

However, do not let us condemn the primitive light source as being unable to help the photographer. Quite the contrary; the primitive light source properly handled can greatly contribute to pictorial expression and to a lifelike representation of certain settings. We all know, for instance, the pictures which show a man lighting his cigarette or the candle on the Christmas tree— indeed, there is hardly a photographer who has not tried his hand on those or similar subjects at one time or another. The candle, especially, offers many pictorial opportunities. Although the eye does not register a halo around the flame, we are now accustomed—undoubtedly through the influence of innumerable paintings—to associate a burning candle with this halo and to consider it an essential—indeed intrinsic—asset to its atmosphere. *The photographer who wishes to produce this glamorous halo effect should use an unbacked plate.* Films and backed negative materials are unsuitable for this purpose.

A candle has also the advantage over similar light sources that it burns off with a comparatively steady flame, and thus facilitates long exposure times. Still, even a long exposure time does not help us to overcome the *excessive* contrast always produced by a primitive light source because of its smallness and the absence of reflected light. It is consequently necessary to give at least one supplementary light which renders detail which otherwise would be lost.

In other words: to make the best of these assets the photographer must look at the primitive light source as just another object in the picture while he produces his main lighting with a proper *photographic* light source.

A picture in which a primitive light source is included needs special lighting treatment and here are a few hints on the subject :

(1) The lighting should be simple.

(2) The lighting should not contradict the pictorial situation.

(3) A primitive light source should only be included in a picture when the pictorial plot warrants it.

(4) When including a primitive light source in a picture one must also show the reason for its existence and the atmosphere surrounding it.

THE SHADOW

Light and shade are for the photographer more than facts of physics, more than questions of technical construction. Light and shade are not merely extraneous agents making things perceptible to vision or helping to create images on negatives, but are the intrinsic forces which give photography justification for its existence. One can go even further and say that the " translation " of light and shade into terms of optical *and* sensorial impressions *is* photography.

It is obvious that this task of photography can only be performed if the photographer is able to control light and shadow, and to apply their possibilities according to his wish. It is also essential that the photographer know by practical experience the many and varied groupings of available light sources, so that he can visualise the intended and final result, before he has started to move even a single lamp.

Here the question arises whether it is advisable to evolve a number of " standard schemes " of lighting which can be employed in turn on different occasions. I am of the opinion that such standard schemes can do more harm than good, for they so often tend to lead to mental inflexibility and to a general mechanisation of technique. Please bear in mind that when in later pages I give certain " light schemes " and examples, these are intended to serve merely as a general guide and not as a ready-made solution for all photographic problems.

TYPES OF SHADOWS

We must first understand what we mean by the term " shadow ". We shall distinguish between the *true shadow* and the *bogus shadow*.

The true shadow—or the cast shadow, to call it by its more common name —is an area from which light is partially or totally eliminated by a more or less opaque obstacle introduced between the light source and the base of projection. Needless to say, the obstacle has to be smaller than the beam of light. Characteristic of the true (cast) shadow is its *dependence on the existence of a light-*
66

obstructing substance: the projection base (background). It will therefore have a definite shape—a shape primarily depending on the form of the subject.

The bogus shadow is an area from which light is partially or totally eliminated. Characteristic of the bogus shadow is that it does *not* depend on a substance, but that it is *merely a matter of tone-gradation* produced by a deterioration of light.

From the psychological point of view, the bogus shadow can have the same effect as the true shadow. *Both* types of shadow are able to evoke thought-associations and create what we call " atmosphere ". Considered from the viewpoint of lighting technique, however, it is imperative that we adhere to the differentiation between the cast true shadow and the bogus shadow. It must be realised that we can control a cast shadow to a far greater extent than a bogus shadow. While the tone, definition, shape and size of a true shadow can be widely influenced by varying methods, the bogus shadow depends to such a degree on the surface-form of the object or on the character of our light source that its construction is more or less incidental.

The next sections make the great adaptability of the cast shadow clearly apparent and demonstrate the different methods of shadow control. But we shall also revert to the bogus shadow, which has its own problems and its individual pictorial significance.

THE TONE OF THE CAST SHADOW

We have to distinguish between a " pure " and a " diluted " shadow. By pure shadow we mean that the shadow is completely black, by diluted shadow it is lightened up to varying degrees. *The smaller the light source and the nearer the shadow-casting object is to the background the " purer " will be the shadow.*

Just hold your outstretched hand between an ordinary lamp and a light surface, *e.g.,* a light table-top. Naturally you will obtain a shadow. Now you will note that when you hold your hand *very* close to the table, the shadow is practically pure, but when you move your hand slightly higher, away from the table, you will obtain a lighter edge around a pure-black shadow nucleus. The pure, inner part is called the *Umbra*, the lighter, outer part the *Penumbra*. Now you will observe that the farther you remove your hand from the table, the larger will become the penumbra and the smaller the umbra, until the hand is so far away that the shadow is totally penumbral. This means that the pure, umbral nucleus has been lost and that all which remains is a shadow which is grey or diluted.

If you now repeat this experiment with a small light source you will see that you can remove your hand much farther away from the table than before and still retain a comparatively pure shadow.

These facts become important when you project a shadow on to a background which is detached from the shadow-casting object. On the other hand,

67

it is plain that they lose a lot of their usefulness for tone-control when the object is connected with the background, as, in this case, the distance between object and projection-base is always comparatively small and the shadow therefore more or less pure.

If we wish to control the tone of a shadow under the latter conditions we must use another method (*i.e., employ a supplementary light*). This second method is the practical one, because it can be more universally employed. It can be used equally well whether the shadow is annexed (*i.e.,* linked up with the shadow-casting substance) or when it is isolated (*i.e.,* detached from the object).

One just has to take a second lamp and lighten the shadow to the desired degree. There are, however, a few points which have to be watched.

First of all, it must be remembered that the second light has in this case the sole purpose of lighting an existing shadow—not producing a new one. It will therefore be necessary either to direct the light from such an angle that no new shadow is produced, or, since this is not always possible, one must use a light source which, by its nature, will not produce a shadow too easily, or in any case only a very faint one. The safest light source is here not a lamp, but a sheet of mat white board which lightens the shadows by reflection only (see p. 42).

In order to avoid misunderstandings I wish to say that there are, of course, occasions when two shadows from one single object are desired—for instance, in order to make a shadow pattern. In that part in which two diluted shadows overlap, the shadow will become more or less pure. This has, however, nothing to do with tone-control, but with composition.

Some may now ask how dark or how light a shadow should be. There is one rule which can be considered valid for most occasions: *the purer the shadow the more predominant, the more diluted the more insignificant will it appear in the picture.* Some people believe that there should be " drawing in the shadow " —that it should be kept light enough to make the structure of the underlying surface still discernible. Good advice as that may be in many cases, it is definitely not good enough to be acclaimed as a rule. The thesis would, first of all, only be applicable to " body-shadows ", and not to fine " line-shadows ". Secondly, it leaves out of account the many expressive possibilities of a heavy silhouette treatment. I am the last person to advocate anything like uncontrolled and meaningless black patches which seem to have no other task in a picture but to disturb the pictorial composition, and consequently to irritate the spectator. At the same time, however, I would suggest that in many cases it is often just the pure shadow, with its extinction of underlying detail, which can evoke in us the sensation of darkness with all its pictorial significance.

DEFINITION OF THE CAST SHADOW

The term shadow-definition refers to either the " hardness " or " softness " of a shadow, meaning whether its *edges* are sharp or fuzzy. Definition depends

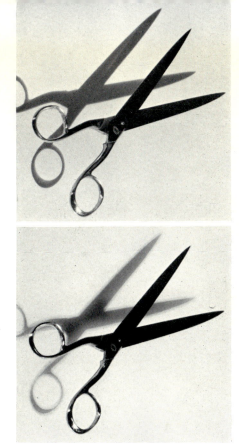

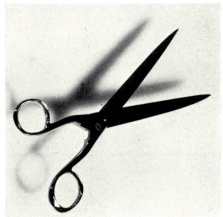

SHADOW DEFINITION. *Top :* spot light producing sharply defined shadows. *Upper centre :* flood leading to a softer type of light. *Lower centre :* diffused flood and diffused shadow. *Bottom :* double lighting means doubling the shadow. If symmetrically arranged, as in this case, a pleasing shadow pattern may be produced.

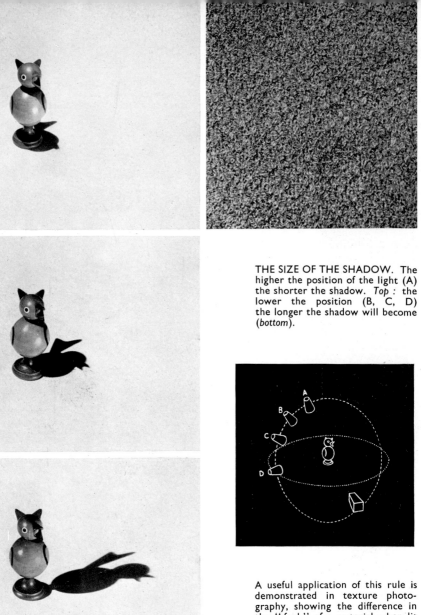

THE SIZE OF THE SHADOW. The higher the position of the light (A) the shorter the shadow. *Top* : the lower the position (B, C, D) the longer the shadow will become (*bottom*).

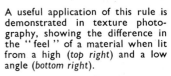

A useful application of this rule is demonstrated in texture photography, showing the difference in the "feel" of a material when lit from a high (*top right*) and a low angle (*bottom right*).

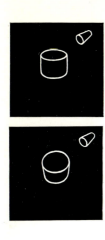

THE SHAPE OF THE SHADOW is essentially influenced by the position of the subject. Even a subject of a comparatively simple outline may produce intricate shadow patterns with its position in relation to the background carefully chosen. Note that the position of the light source has been left unchanged in all the four pictures.

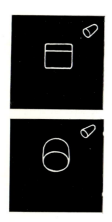

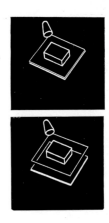

ISOLATING THE SHADOW. The subject is placed on a sheet of glass. By lengthening the distance between the glass and the actual background, the shadow projected on to this background is being isolated from the subject. It is easy to see that pictures can be obtained where the shadow has actually been moved out of the angle of camera vision or can be trimmed off the print.

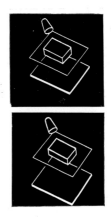

on the same factors as the tone of a shadow (see p. 67): firstly, on the *size and construction of the light source*, and secondly on the *distance of the obstructive substance from the projection-base.*

This implies that, having these two factors under one's control, the definition of a shadow can be produced according to one's own free will and intention; it is not the accidental outcome of existing lighting conditions which cannot be modified. It now becomes apparent how important it is to take the greatest care in choosing the right type of lamp for the job. It has already been mentioned (p. 67) that the smaller the light source the better defined is the shadow. We have also seen (p. 31) that the carbon-arc spot-light is for this reason the most suitable light source to employ when a clear-cut shadow is required. A soft shadow can be produced by employing a lamp with a comparatively extensive filament design fixed in a broad and shallow reflector.

The second factor influencing shadow-definition is the distance between the object casting the shadow and the projection-base. The nearer the object is to the projection-base the sharper will be the edges of the shadow, and *vice versa.*

Choose an object which promises to give a simple but impressive shadow pattern (e.g., a piece of wire netting), and move it slowly to and fro between light source and projection-base. Observe well and make notes on lighting employed, distances, etc., and then repeat the experiment with other light sources. You will find the comparison of your notes both absorbing and interesting, all the more so as the quality of the shadow is not only important for composition but also accentuates to a certain degree the character of the subject by which it is cast.

For instance, visualise a pair of scissors. We are accustomed to associate them with sharpness—the keenness of the blades. It is obvious that, if we wish to include the shadow of the scissors in the picture, we must present it as being well defined, with the sharp edge intrinsic to the subject. Wilful diffusion on the shadow in this case would result in an effect which would deprive the subject of one of its characteristic attributes.

SHAPE AND SIZE OF A CAST SHADOW

While the definition of a shadow depends on the kind of light source and on the distance of the obstructive substance from the projection surface, the shape and size of a shadow depend on the following three factors: (1) *distance of object to base of projection.* (2) *Relative position of light source (angle of light-incidence) and angle of object to projection-base.* (3) *Surface-form of projection-base,* i.e., *if the base is plain, convex or concave.* Let us take these points one by one.

(1) The first thing to be realised is that the distance between object and projection-base and the distance between lamp and object can only influence the *size* of the shadow—not its shape. This means that there are three ways of altering the size of a shadow: first to introduce a larger object of exactly

I
73

the same shape into the same position as the original shadow-casting obstacle— leaving the projection-base unmoved; secondly to move the light source farther away from the subject without altering the angle of light-incidence and the position of the object; thirdly to move the projection-base farther away from the object. *The greater the distance between object and projection-base the larger will be the shadow.* It is obvious that the smallest possible size of a shadow is the size of the object which produces it.

(2) The relative positions of object and projection-base, as well as the angle of light-incidence, influence the shape *and* the size of the shadow simultaneously. One can alter size *and* shape of a shadow in two ways: either by *altering the position of the object in relation to the background, without moving the light source— or by altering the angle of light-incidence without altering the position of object or background.*

The first method must necessarily be employed when it is impossible to move the light source. This method also produces a greater number of different shadow-forms. The second method has, however, the advantage that it facilitates more subtle changes and slight differentiations than does the first, which tends to alter the shape of the shadow rather too drastically.

There is the classical rule that *if the light falls at an angle of 45° the length of a shadow is equal to the height of the object. The larger the angle, the shorter becomes the shadow,* and *vice versa.* This means that the longest shadow is produced by a light-incidence of approximately 1°, the shortest shadow by lighting directly from the top, *i.e.,* from an angle of 90°.

(3) The third factor determining the size and shape of a shadow is the surface-form of the background on to which the shadow is projected (*i.e.,* whether it is plain, concave or convex). The influence which the surface-form of the projection-base (or background) has on the shape of a shadow is negligible, but the size (especially the length) of a shadow can be altered by it quite drastically. The method of altering the surface-form of the background is chiefly of theoretical interest—occasions for its successul practical application are somewhat rare.

It will therefore suffice to know that: *A concave projection-base always shortens a shadow. A convex projection-base may either shorten or lengthen the shadow, this being dependent on the grade and kind of bend. The shape of the shadow adjusts itself to the bend of the projection-base.*

DOMINANCE OF CAST SHADOWS

Here again it must be realised that " form of shadow " is not merely a consequence of physical laws having a bearing on aesthetic considerations, such as pictorial composition. No; the form of a shadow is an essential means of enabling the photographer to express a certain message in his picture and to get it over to the spectator. The practical importance of the implications of this point must not be under-rated.

74

For instance, allowing for the exception to the rule, it is obvious that the larger the shadow the more important is the rôle it plays in the picture. It is also plain that, the larger the shadow in comparison with the object which casts it, the more will it dominate the object. This statement is not quite so straightforward as it may seem at a first glance, for the dominance of a shadow can be of two kinds—concrete or abstract. The first is perceptible by vision, the second only by imagination.

Concrete dominance is created by the fact that the space covered by the shadow is comparatively extensive; in consequence the spectator will acknowledge the shadow as a unit of special pictorial importance. This applies specially to texture-photography, which is nothing but the wilful exaggeration of the shadow element by means of an acute and well-defined angle-lighting. The rendering of photographic texture is achieved by elongating the individual shadow particles cast by the surface texture of the object to such an extent that their size is out of proportion to the one created and perceived under ordinary lighting conditions.

Abstract dominance rests in the " dramatic " quality of the shadow. Everyone can visualise, for instance, how a silhouette lifts the pictorial subject out of humdrum reality into the region of the unreal, how the shadow of a man in a raincoat cast on to a brick wall can convert a quite ordinary pictorial situation into a murder story, and how the gruesome effect can still be magnified by elongating the shadow.

THE BOGUS SHADOW

We have seen (p. 66) that, while the cast (true) shadow depends on a light-obstructing substance, the bogus shadow is nothing but an absence of light caused by a bend in an object's surface or by the limited range of illumination from the artificial-light source.

To illustrate the first type of bogus shadow we merely have to visualise a face on which there is a typical play of light and shade. The shadow cast by the nose is obviously a true shadow. But the shadow on the cheek is a bogus shadow—a mere absence of light. Similarly any unilluminated part of a sphere (or rounded object) is a bogus shadow, while the shaded area cast by that sphere (or object) upon its background is a true shadow.

The bogus shadow is instrumental in rendering form. *The softer its edge the softer and rounder will the object appear; the harder its edge the more angular the result.* The degree of hardness of the shadow edge is determined first by the form of the object itself, and secondly by the quality of the light. For instance: the roundness of a face lends itself better to angular shadow-forms than the roundness of a sphere, and the soft light of a flood produces softer forms than the hard light propagated by a spot-light lamp.

The second type of bogus shadow can best be illustrated by projecting a spot of light upon a flat surface. We shall then see that *the area outside the field*

75

of illumination appears to be dark—" in shadow ". Here the difference between the cast shadow and the bogus shadow becomes obvious. The definition of the bogus shadow can be controlled by the choice of the illuminating lamp; needless to repeat that a spot-light gives a harder light than a flood and that, when using a flood, the distance between light source and projection-base has a strong bearing on the effect.

The shape of this second type of bogus shadow depends entirely on the angle at which the light meets the projection-base. When the lamp shines upon it from in front, the shadow-area will encompass a round area of light, while a spot-light placed near the background and shining upon it at a very oblique angle produces two shadow areas distinctly separated by a beam of light, the edges of which run more or less parallel.

In practice we shall soon learn how the bogus shadow presents itself in the picture sometimes merely as a small, incidental unit and sometimes as the planned dynamic base of the picture.

THE ANNEXED CAST SHADOW

A shadow is " annexed " when it is *cast by an object which is linked up with the projection-base,* i.e., if the shadow-producing substance stands or leans directly on its background or is naturally attached to it.

Examples of an annexed shadow are, for instance, the shadow of the nose or the texture-shadows in a piece of fabric. It is obvious that these types of shadow—resulting from the moulding of the subject's surface—can never be converted into isolated shadow forms. There are other kinds of annexed shadows—for example, those produced by a vase standing on a table or a figure leaning against a pillar—which can be made into isolated shadows easily enough. One has just to lift the vase up from the table or place the figure a little distance away from the background.

It is typical of the annexed shadow that the spectator takes its existence for granted. The spectator hardly notes its presence in a picture as long as the shadow is not strengthened and individualised to such an extent that he recognises it as something out of the ordinary, something he is not accustomed to seeing in everyday life.

The reason for this is obvious: everyone knows that whenever an object is lighted it must provide a shadow somewhere—unless the light-beam is too small to envelop the object. Our memory is not impressed by those few instances where the shadow evades our mechanical vision on account of some abnormal diffusion of the light source, purely reflective backgrounds or other similar influences.

It follows that the photographer has to accentuate strongly the form of the annexed shadow if he wishes to lift it out of its Cinderella existence. But here a warning might not be misplaced. The flexibility of technique which enables us to " mould " shadow and raise it from relative insignificance to a highly

76

expressive and creative agent must not be abused in an irresponsible manner. The artificial bolstering up of the shadow must not be misused for the sake of cheap effects, nor for purely " formal " reasons. This is done much too often. Indeed, photography today tends to give too much importance to purely ornamental shadow forms, and to dwell in an exuberance of pattern for its own sake.

This habit of presenting shadow as an aesthetic superficiality must lead to a point when the spectator will recognise it merely as a shallow, commonplace fabrication. Photography will thus lose one of the few means by which it can hope to emancipate itself from its mechanical, solely representational status.

Especially regarding still-life photography I advise the student to take he annexed shadow for just what it really is—the companion to the main object illustrated. He should realise that the shadow should help to make the best of the object, not think that the only excuse for the object's presence in the picture is its faculty of producing an " interesting shadow ". After all, it is the purpose of all pictures either to portray objects, animate or inanimate, or to express the photographer's attitude to them—form and composition being subordinated to these ends.

THE ISOLATED SHADOW

A shadow is " isolated " when it is *projected by an object which is separated from its background*, i.e., when the shadow-casting substance is placed some distance away from the projection-base.

The " isolated " shadow presents to the photographer technical possibilities which an annexed shadow is unable to give.   Here are a few examples:

Although an isolated shadow may be optically perceived as if it is " grown on " to the subject, it is in fact a distance away from it. This *enables the photographer to give additional lighting to the subject without touching the shadow*, and therefore without altering its tone-value. In particular, symmetrical outline effects can be produced by means of highlights around the subject, without the loss of any purity and definition in the shadow; were the shadow annexed to the subject this would not be possible because the lights which create these highlight effects must then also touch the background to which the object is attached, and thus either produce a new shadow pattern or lighten the main shadow-unit, or both.

The detachment of the object from its background also makes it *possible to alter the tone-value of the background* without at the same time altering the tone-value of the object.   This is, however, not all.   The isolation of the shadow from its substance offers still further advantages.

We have seen (p. 73) that the only method of altering the size of a shadow, without simultaneously altering its shape or the size of the shadow-casting object, is to move the object farther away from the projection-base. From this it follows that the isolated shadow treatment not only enables us *to alter the size of the shadow itself according to our wish*, but also to alter the relation between object and shadow in respect of size and pictorial (or psychological) importance.

THE SILHOUETTE SHADOW

The isolated shadow presents itself in its purest form in the " silhouette ". Here the pictorial detachment from the object is complete and the shadow takes on a life of its own; it is the shadow—not the object itself—which tells the story in the picture.

The silhouette tends to evoke a certain feeling of unreality. This statement should not be misinterpreted. One is too easily tempted to associate with the term unreality a mystical gloom or a sinister, fathomless symbolism. It should, however, be realised that this constitutes only one side of the Unreal. Gay and joyful exhilaration can also be lifted into the sphere of unreality without its light-heartedness being lost in the process.

Silhouettes can be cast either by any object which lends itself to this purpose, or by a flat (cardboard) mask which represents certain settings, such as a window with flower-pots, a motor-car, a ship, etc. Besides these naturalistic subjects one can choose to cut masks which represent merely some kind of geometrical pattern.

A pure and well-defined image is usually expected of a silhouette and it is for this reason that a *spot-light or a similar light source should be employed* for its production. For the benefit of the professional photographer special projectors have been marketed into which masks can be inserted between the projector lamp and a lens.

A further point to be particularly remembered is that *the lighting of the foreground unit must never touch the background* on to which the silhouette has been cast. Stray lighting will weaken the silhouette image considerably, sometimes nearly to extinction, or the shadows of the foreground unit may interfere with the silhouette. It is therefore advisable to employ spot-lights and *not* flood-lamps for the lighting of the foreground unit.

Silhouette-shadows can also be produced in an entirely different way, by projecting the shadow image from behind a translucent background. When employing this method we have to remember, firstly, that the object is to be placed very near to the background and, secondly, that the light source be a good distance away from the object but, at the same time, completely hidden by it. Only then can we achieve a clear-cut shadow image and also a background which is *evenly* lit. The method of projecting a shadow in this way has two advantages. It produces an image free of distortion and is also more convenient for the amateur. He who may either be restricted in working space or has no suitable wall space can overcome his difficulties by taking a large linen sheet which he fastens into a door frame and by placing object and light source in one room and his camera in the other. Needless to state,

78

there must be no other kind of illumination in either room while the photograph is being taken.

Background silhouettes must not be confused with what is commonly called " background-projection ". This term does not refer to shadow-projection at all, but to a technique by which lantern slides are projected on to a screen. The fundamental difference between those two kinds of projection technique lies in the fact that " background-projection " (see p. 63) aims at a realistic, three-dimensional effect, while the silhouette can never create more than a plain, *two*-dimensional impression.

OTHER KINDS OF ISOLATED CAST SHADOW

We have seen that the silhouette is the prototype of the isolated shadow because it is isolated from the object to such an extent that the object is entirely excluded from the picture. Not every isolated shadow is, however, detached to this extent. It can stand—pictorially—" beside " the object, or even be partially overlapped by it, so that it vanishes, more or less, behind the shadow-producing substance.

Now, it might be argued that such a shadow which seems to be connected with its subject should not be called " isolated ", as it has the same effect on the spectator as any ordinary " annexed " shadow. It must, however, be realised that even if a differentiation may not seem necessary from the viewpoint of final effect, it is essential with regard to the production of a photograph.

SHADOW-FREE TREATMENTS

Shadow-free photography describes two entirely different lighting treatments. The *first* method aims at an *avoidance of cast* (true) *shadows on the object as well as on its background*. It will be found applied mainly to " high-key " portraiture and nude photography. The *second* method aims at the *complete elimination of cast* (true) *shadows on the background only*, and is widely used for the normal kind of portrait and figure study and also for special types of still-life photography.

In order to avoid confusion between these two treatments, we shall describe the first as " shadowless photography " and the second as " shadow-free background photography ". Both have their individual application, approach and technique. It is therefore essential to investigate the two groups of shadow-free photography separately.

SHADOWLESS PHOTOGRAPHY

A high-key photograph is a picture in which light tones are dominating and in which as little shadow as possible should appear. In principle, high-key photographs can be produced by ordinary lighting methods so long as heavy

79

shadows are few or otherwise sufficiently diluted by supplementary lighting. It is obvious, however, that the most typical examples of high-key lighting will be created by employing a technique which in itself excludes cast shadows.

Those photographers who claim shadowless photography to be the " ideal " photographic method aim at the following results: *First* they wish to convey two-dimensional instead of three-dimensional effects; *secondly* they endeavour to obtain the greatest possible number of subtle half-tones by sacrificing contrast; *thirdly* they wish to achieve modelling without the help of cast shadows.

High-key pictures created by shadowless photography undoubtedly have their merits. They convey a certain ethereal quality and deftness which no other method is able to achieve. But it is a definitely short-sighted view to acclaim shadowless portrait and figure photography as the most " pure " form of photographic expression. Admittedly shadowless lighting produces the best possible literal reproduction in a two-dimensional manner, but it would indeed be depressing to have to acknowledge that literal representation in a two-dimensional style is all that can be asked of photography. It will hardly do either to see in the rendering of the greatest possible number of half-tones the true and only purpose of photography.

Every photographer is entitled to use any lighting treatment he sees fit so long as it fulfils his purpose and gives aesthetic satisfaction. We each have our own way of looking at things and appreciating them. There is as much justification for producing a photograph exclusively in heavy dark tones as for producing one exclusively in delicately light greys and whites—as long as each of them suits its particular subject. There are as well plenty of themes to justify a bold treatment showing a clash between high-light and darkest shadow; although it may, on most occasions, be desirable to have a certain amount of " drawing in the shadows " or sometimes even a complete lack of pure shadows.

Shadowless lighting is fully justified as an important photographic method— just as many other methods are. At the same time we always have to remember that it should be used only in connection with a high-key model and a high-key theme and not merely because the photographer happens to consider it " pretty ".

Every enthusiast of shadowless photography seems to have, at first glance, a technique of his own. One recommends a single flood reflector fitted with a projector bulb for the main light source, another uses a most complicated " Ring-light unit " consisting of a number of filament bulbs fitted into a special circular flood arrangement surrounding the front of the camera. When we come to investigate the seemingly varying methods more closely, we soon find that in practice the general principles are alike and that the variance between one technique and another is only slight—indeed merely a question of mechanical detail.

The general principles are: (1) *The light source (flood) to be as near to the lens as is practicable in order to make the line of light-incidence coincide with the*

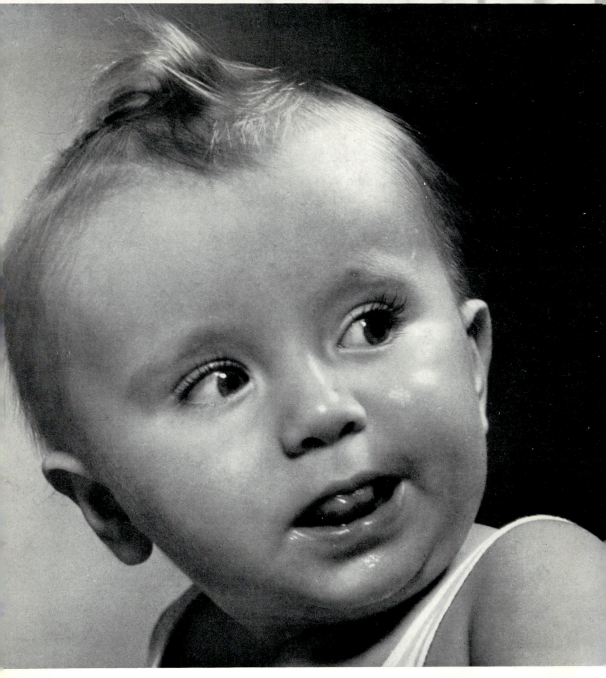

LIGHTING AS A MEANS TO NATURAL MODELLING. Artificial lighting is employed here in its most unobtrusive manner. It does not appear as such at all, but just helps to depict the head in its natural roundness. Phot : *Torkel Korling, Chicago.*

81

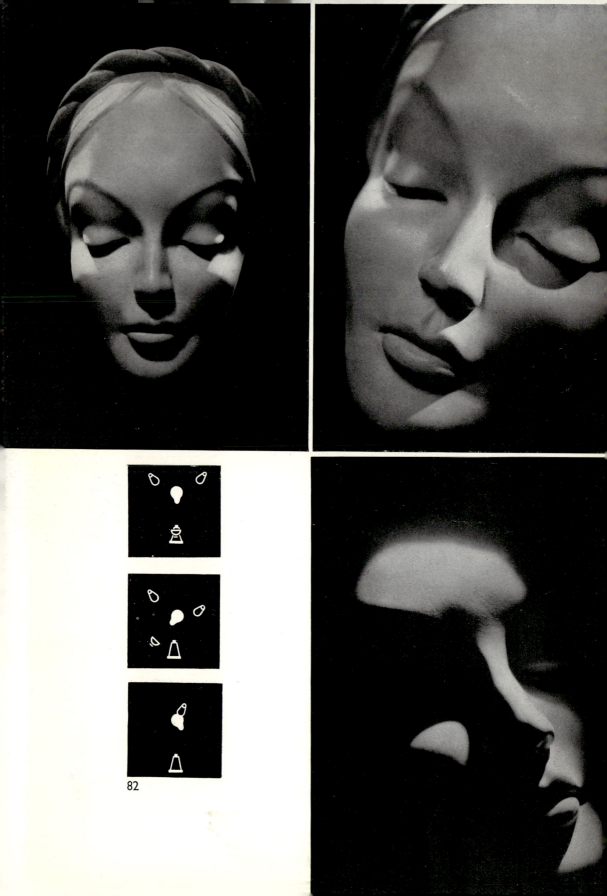

82

PICTORIALLY CREATIVE LIGHTING. *On page 82.* The choice of the lamp and its positioning enable the photographer to bring to almost every face a story of its own. Phot : *W. Nurnberg, London.*

TWO-DIMENSIONAL LIGHTING. Counterpart of the natural style of lighting aimed at round modelling is the high key style of widely diffused front lighting, creating an almost chalk sketch effect. Phot : *Jan de Meyere, Stockholm.*

LIGHTING WITHOUT BACKGROUND SHADOW. The use of a glass base and a removed background leads to isolation of the shadow and leaves the subject apparently suspended in an undefined space. This is a successful method of lighting for still life and commercial work. Phot : *Alexander, London.*

line of camera-vision. (2) *The elevation of camera and lamp to be slightly lower than the eye-level of a sitting person.* (3) *The sitter to be a good distance away from the background.* (4) *The background to be kept white by a separate illumination.*

The result is a complete absence of *cast* shadows on object and background. It must, however, be realised that this positioning of the light source produces a certain amount of light deterioration around the outline of the object. This presents itself as a narrow bogus shadow, helping to separate the image from the light tone of the background. To eliminate these narrow rim-shadows we must employ a *soft three-quarter backlighting* from both sides of the object.

Judging from the material available and from our experiments it seems that this particular technique is only successful when employed in connection with either full-face or full-profile positions. If no head is included in the picture (when photographing a torso) three-quarter positions can also be successfully tackled in this way.

Soft negative materials should be used in order to create good modelling without the help of cast shadows; we also have to guard against any excessive over-exposures which would clog up the subtle half-tones.

SHADOW-FREE BACKGROUND PHOTOGRAPHY

This method means nothing more than the removal of the background-shadow from the picture by isolating the shadow from its substance. There are occasions when the absence of a shadow on the background is an asset. The main purposes to which shadow-free background photography can be applied are threefold: *for " autonomous " background treatment; for imitation cut-out aiming at better outline definition of the object; and for more successful rendering of certain materials.*

Let us first consider in which way we can best get rid of a shadow from the picture.

If the shadow is annexed this is difficult, although theoretically possible. Indeed, but for one exception, I do not consider the complete elimination of an annexed shadow as a practical (or even desirable) possibility. The one exception mentioned is provided by the *black background.* By taking black silk velvet for our background material the shadow is made practically invisible because of the property of the material of absorbing light to such a high degree. No other material than black silk-velvet is suitable for a complete suppression of shadow. Black paper or other kinds of black fabric do not lend themselves to this purpose, as they are not sufficiently light-absorbent (see p. 19).

As soon as one wishes to obtain a background which is lighter than " pitch " black, the *only way to eradicate the shadow would be to light it away;* that means to flood the shadow with such an amount of light that it is no longer perceptible to the vision. This method is, however, most unsatisfactory, for the flooding of the shadow will also affect, in most cases, the object, thus making it appear unplastic or textureless. Now, it might be suggested that the light which is destined to eradicate the shadow could be " spotted " to such an extent and in such a manner that the object and the surrounding background parts are not touched by the light-beam. Theoretically this sounds feasible, but in practice it will be found that it is hardly ever possible to make light behave in such a perfect manner.

For this reason a different method of shadow-elimination had to be found, a method *not* aiming at a " lighting-away " of the shadow. It was found in *excluding the background-shadow from the picture space.* Now, it will be obvious that this can only be made possible if the shadow is completely isolated from its substance and shifted far enough so that it no longer appears inside the picture's frame.

This method presents no special difficulties; if it were possible—as we have seen in the production of the silhouette shadow—to separate object and shadow to such an extent that the only unit included in the picture was the shadow, it is only logical that using the same means, it should be also possible to retain the object as the sole pictorial unit.

Here are two facts which have to be remembered:

The farther the object is placed away from the background the easier it is to produce a shadow-free photograph.

The larger (wider) the angle between the light-beam and the line of camera-vision the easier is it to exclude the shadow from the pictorial frame, the smaller this angle the more difficult will it become. If the line of camera-vision coincides with the line of light, a pictorial separation will be impossible.

When photographing an object *standing in front* of a background, shadow-free background photography is easily accomplished. The process becomes slightly more complicated when photographing an object which must—by its nature—*lie on* a background. In the latter case we may have to *substitute a glass plate for the original background* in order to serve as a base for the object. By fixing the glass plate—which now carries the object—well above the original background we are now able to reproduce an isolated shadow which can be excluded from the picture space in the usual manner. This glass plate should be supported on the corners only. Bulky supports on the side would easily throw additional shadows across the background. The glass plate must be of the finest quality and of course its size adequate to the needs of the picture. If too small a size is chosen, it can easily happen that the edges of the glass plate cast shadows across the camera's field of vision.

The first application of *autonomous background treatment* is that in which the background is to be kept clear not only of shadows cast from the picture's subject, but also from any stray lighting originating from the lights illuminating the subject. By this method one obtains a completely blank background space which can now be treated autonomously, *i.e.*, quite for itself without interfering with the lighting on the main subject.

This method is particularly used when " background projection " is to be employed or if one wishes to " paint " the background with light; in por-

86

traiture it is most useful because it enables the photographer either to individualise or to generalise the background element and to accentuate or repress it in relation to the foreground unit.

In still-life photography it may become necessary to give different exposure times to foreground and background. The complete separation of foreground and background units achieved by means of shadow-free photography makes it, for instance, possible to expose a dark object in the foreground proportionally longer than its white background, thus avoiding " lack of drawing " in the dark object or an over-exposure of the white background. The value of this technical flexibility is obvious, and the student will find out in his own experiments that this specific aspect of shadow-free photography will help him to overcome problems which otherwise have to be shelved as unsolved.

The second way of application is the *imitation cut-out*. It will be found most useful in connection with still-life photography.

If you look at a catalogue illustrating—let us say—technical instruments, you are bound to run across illustrations which stand well defined in the middle of white space and in which the object is presented without a shadow annexed to it. These effects are usually produced by retouching. Either the background around the object has been covered up with opaque paint on the negative (" blocking out ") or colour has been applied around the outlines of the object on the photographic print before being used for blockmaking.

The same result can be achieved by eliminating the background shadow by means of a glass plate (see p. 72). In this way every tone of grey, as well as pure white and black, can easily be produced without necessitating any retouching on the print later on. But this is not the only merit of this method. Its main advantage lies in the fact that the object—being placed well away from the background—can be lit from *all* angles, thus facilitating an excellent definition of its outline and a plastic rendering of its form while the background—being undisturbed by shadows—retains its smooth flatness of tone.

The complete removal of background shadows from the picture-space can be of great help to the photographer in his endeavours to reproduce the *shape or the texture* of certain products or materials more faithfully. Especially when tackling transparent matter—glass, cellophane, celluloid—shadow-free background photography is most useful.

The absence of shadow tends to give a certain ethereal quality to a transparent body by removing the feeling of gravity which is always connected with matter, and by putting in its place a feeling of lightness.

But also from a purely photo-technical point of view the shadow-free method has great advantages when photographing transparent objects. Just to give an example, excellent definition of glassware can be achieved by concentrating the lighting solely on the background, as this method eliminates any possible reflection on the surface of the glass object. At the same time there will be no background shadow which could interfere with the sometimes delicate outline and structure of the glass. The latter fact applies especially to cut-glass.

87

IV

THE APPLICATION OF LIGHTING

LIGHT AND SHADOW AS APPLIED TO FACE AND FIGURE

I have promised not to confront the reader with a set of rigid rules and lighting schemes. The reason for this will now become obvious. When, for instance, watching a human face we find that its form and whole appearance change drastically with every single curve of the head. Sunlight falling upon a face or figure does so without taking the wishes of the photographer into consideration. The photographer has therefore to move his model about until the light shines on it in just the way he wants it to shine. Needless to say that when working with artificial-light sources the shifting is not done to persons, but to lamps.

The term portraiture describes two different kinds of photographic activity —either photographing a person for the sake of achieving a likeness or the subjective interpretation of the sitter. This second type of portrait can be a purely subjective effort, and the task of such a study appears to be fulfilled so long as the photographer himself thinks that he has achieved what he set out to do.

It is obvious that the ordinary commercial portrait, aiming at creating a likeness which is appreciated not only by the sitter himself but also by his entire family, friends and relations, greatly restricts the photographer in his choice of lighting. He will definitely not make a success of his job if he " lights " a lady, who wishes to look twenty years younger, in such a way that she looks twenty years older, through employing hard spot-light effects, which meet the face at an oblique angle and bring all the wrinkles and skin texture in an exaggerated fashion. If he lights a gentleman who is very proud of his smart appearance, from underneath, so that he looks in a full-face view like an under-nourished bulldog, he will also make himself unpopular. If, on the other hand, the photographer " sees " the gentleman in question as an under-nourished bulldog and the afore-mentioned lady with the skin of a hippopotamus, and experiences the inner urge to announce these visions to the world, he is of course quite free to use lighting which emphasises those points. He should not be amazed, however—being an amateur and a relative of his models

90

—if he is cut out from their wills or—being a professional photographer—if his " artistic " efforts are slammed round his ears.

It must be appreciated that, quite apart from questions of expediency, certain types of lighting are more suitable for profile, other types for full-face views, and I think that the reader will see best what can and cannot be done by basing the following examination not on the setting of the light sources, but on the various positions of the person to be photographed.

THE PROFILE

A face seen in profile does not convey much actual expression. You see only one eye, and this only from a side view. The curve of the lips is only indicated, and the whole attitude of the sitter is turned away from the camera, and therefore also from the beholder of the picture.

A profile study is therefore only seldom suitable for bringing out the character of the person portrayed, and never suitable for establishing that certain kind of personal contact we so often perceive when a person looks at us. It can, however, help the photographer to bring out facial characteristics when these are to be found in the face's contour. Furthermore, that certain air of detachment intrinsic to the profile position can be utilised for creating certain ethereal facial effects. Another advantage of a profile picture is that it often hides faults, thus flattering the sitter.

If we consider these main purposes of a profile picture, we can easily visualise the kind of lighting we have to employ in connection with the profile study. It will be obvious that if we wish to accentuate the outline of the face, we have to accentuate this outline by some means of lighting. There are two ways of doing this: either by a light contour against a darker background, or by a darker face-outline against a lighter background. The second method (dark outline against light background) is a rather old-fashioned mode and achieves a somewhat flat image of a two-dimensional character. The more modern method—accentuating the face's contour by means of a high light—gives the photographer a better chance to modify the lighting according to his wishes, and also lends itself to a greater variety of supplementary light effects.

Here are the main kinds of lighting treatment to be employed for a face in a full profile position.

PURE SILHOUETTE

Especially suitable for " ghost " effects or any other occasions where the object of the illustration forbids the showing of realistic details.

Basic light: Floods on background only, creating a flat white tone all over.
Supplementary light: None.
Special remarks: It becomes apparent that by lighting the background only and leaving the object completely untouched by light, an extreme contrast of black and white is achieved. The effectiveness of a pure silhouette relies on a " telling " and easily distinguishable outline of the sitter.

Suitable for ethereal effects in connection with the photography of young girls and women, also for " film star " effects in connection with male portraiture.

Basic light: Flood on background.
Supplementary Light: One diffused flood from front position of lamp near the camera but on the side to which sitter is facing. Elevation of lamp the same as elevation of the head.
Second Supplementary Light: Can be employed for slightly " picking-up " dark hair. This should be done by a flood coming directly from the top, and must not touch the face of the sitter.
Special Remarks: It is obvious that the luminosity of the face must be less than the luminosity of the background. The tone value of the face is easily controlled by moving the lamp either nearer to or farther away from the sitter.

DARK OUTLINE-LIGHTING

An antiquated method still frequently used in commercial portrait studies. This kind of technique creates a very impersonal and flat effect which is without vigour and does not give the photographer scope for interpreting his own ideas. A dark outline profile can seldom go beyond producing a literal likeness.

Basic Light: Flood on background producing a white or grey tone.
Supplementary Light: Flood preferably fitted with a projector bulb to be placed beside the camera, but on the side which is opposite to the one which the sitter is facing. The flood should be elevated to eye-level of sitter.
Special Remarks: The luminosity on the face produced by the supplementary light should equal approximately the luminosity on the background.

RIM LIGHT

For the accentuation of well-featured profiles aiming again at a two-dimensional effect. If the rim profile lighting is used without supplementary lighting it produces a very dramatic effect but is unsuitable for the creation of a likeness. If the rim light, on the other hand, is supplemented by further lighting, this technique can be employed for normal portrait work and character studies.

Basic Lighting: The spot-light is placed on the side to which the sitter is facing. It is placed slightly behind the sitter, and its elevation is overhead so as to produce a light which runs along the face's contour without touching that side of the face facing the camera.
Supplementary Light: For very dramatic effects: none. For other purposes: a spot-light at approximately the same position as the basic light, but on the other side of the sitter, thus creating a rim light on the top and back of the head. This spot-light should be slightly more diffused than the basic light.
Second Supplementary Light: Diffused flood from that side of camera which conforms with the side to which the sitter is looking.

92

THE PROFILE. Silhouettes are uncompromising pictures. They can be very characteristic with sitters of characteristic profiles. They can be made charming and witty by finding the appropriate pose. They do not, however, offer much variability in the lighting arrangements. Phot : *M. Salier, London*.

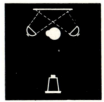

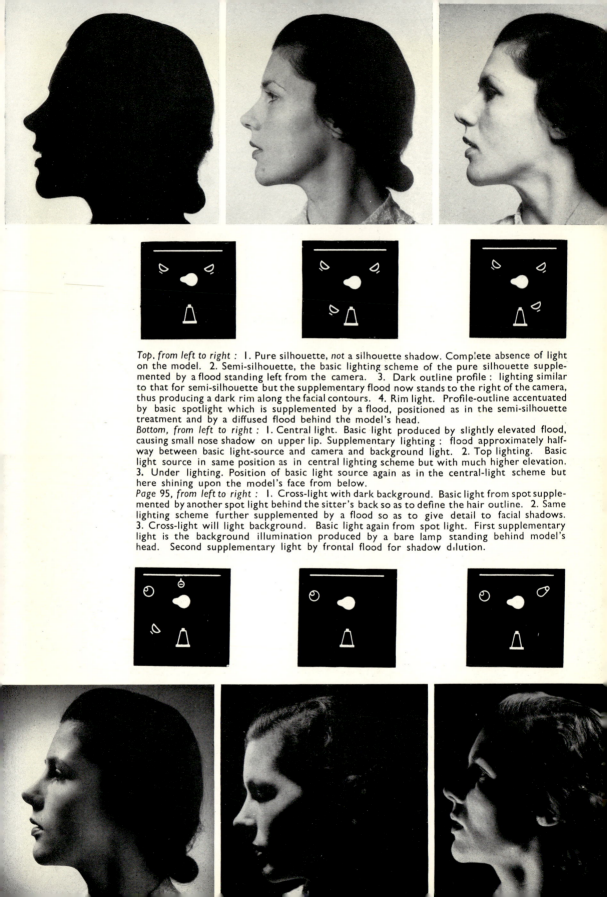

Top, from left to right : 1. Pure silhouette, *not* a silhouette shadow. Complete absence of light on the model. 2. Semi-silhouette, the basic lighting scheme of the pure silhouette supplemented by a flood standing left from the camera. 3. Dark outline profile : lighting similar to that for semi-silhouette but the supplementary flood now stands to the right of the camera, thus producing a dark rim along the facial contours. 4. Rim light. Profile-outline accentuated by basic spotlight which is supplemented by a flood, positioned as in the semi-silhouette treatment and by a diffused flood behind the model's head.

Bottom, from left to right : 1. Central light. Basic light produced by slightly elevated flood, causing small nose shadow on upper lip. Supplementary lighting : flood approximately half-way between basic light-source and camera and background light. 2. Top lighting. Basic light source in same position as in central lighting scheme but with much higher elevation. 3. Under lighting. Position of basic light source again as in the central-light scheme but here shining upon the model's face from below.

Page 95, from left to right : 1. Cross-light with dark background. Basic light from spot supplemented by another spot light behind the sitter's back so as to define the hair outline. 2. Same lighting scheme further supplemented by a flood so as to give detail to facial shadows. 3. Cross-light will light background. Basic light again from spot light. First supplementary light is the background illumination produced by a bare lamp standing behind model's head. Second supplementary light by frontal flood for shadow dilution.

On page 96, top left : Portrait Anton Walbrook.   Normal central lighting.   Flood produces dilution of the shadow parts.   Phot : Alexander, London.   Top right: glamour lighting.   Basic light from

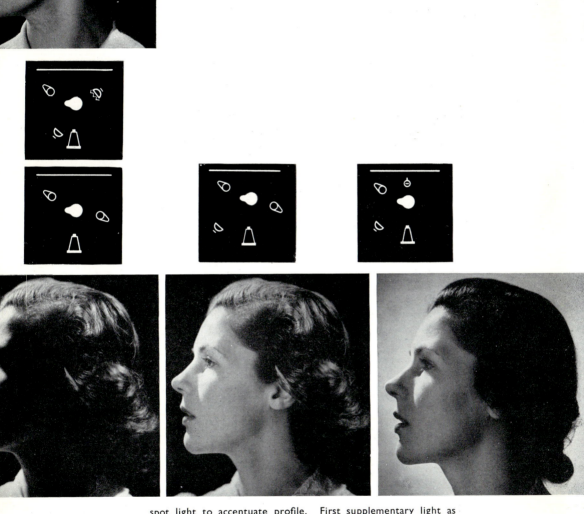

spot light to accentuate profile.   First supplementary light as background illumination behind the model's head.   Second supplementary light for overhead spot effect.   Flood for general lighting.   Phot : W. Nurnberg, London.   Right : basic light is modified cross lighting produced by a spot.   The supplementary light makes use of the ear to cast a pronounced light and shade pattern.   The second supplementary light is a flood diluting the shadow slightly.   Phot : W. Nurnberg, London.

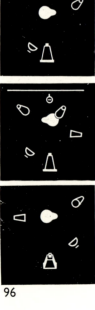

96

THREE-QUARTER FACE. The dark outline profile technique is an unorthodox treatment for three-quarter face and should be used with care. Not every face can stand up to the over-emphasised foreshortening of the side away from the camera and to the resulting accentuation of the nose line. Phot : *Eric Balg, Berlin.*

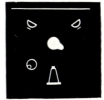

Top : Semi-silhouette. Basic light is the background illumination. First supplementary light : flood left from the camera, elevation such as to avoid cast shadows on the face and to give the face a slightly darker tone than that of the background. Second supplementary light : spot light from behind the sitter for hair lighting.

Bottom : The three types of central lighting. *Left* : Normal central light. Basic light : frontal flood slightly elevated. First supplementary light : spot from behind the sitter ; second supplementary light : background illumination produced by a bare lamp behind the model. Third supplementary light : flood near the basic light source at an elevation which avoids further cast shadows on the face. *Centre* : Top-lighting. Basic light : highly elevated central light. First supplementary light : spot for hair definition as before. Second supplementary light : frontal flood for shadow diffussion. *Right* : Under-lighting. Basic light : central lighting from a very low angle ; supplemented by a back-spot.

On page 99, *top* : Two types of cross-light treatment. *Left* : Light-triangle pointing towards camera. Basic light in orthodox lamp position supplemented by a spot and a frontal flood. *Right* : light-triangle pointing towards background. Basic light produced

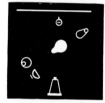

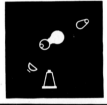

by spot near the camera. First supplementary light : back spot. Second supplementary light : background illumination. Third supplementary light : frontal flood for shadow diffusion.

Bottom : Side-lighting. *Left* : One-sided side-lighting : basic lighting by spot illuminating far side of model's face. First supplementary light : back-spot. Second supplementary light : frontal flood, lighting up the near side of the face. Third supplementary light : background illumination. *Right* : Double-side lighting.

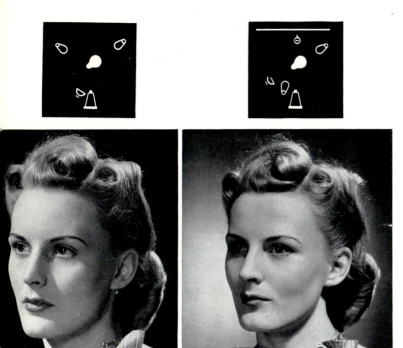

Basic light as before by spot. First supplementary light : elevated
spot-light illuminating the cheek facing the camera and accentuating
the cheek bone. Second supplementary light : frontal flood ;
third supplementary light : background illumination.

On page 100, top left : double side lighting. Phot : *W. Nurnberg,
London (by courtesy of Alfred Pemberton, Ltd.). Top right :* cross light
treatment supplemented by rim light on back and top of head.
Light treatment of background. Phot : *W. Nurnberg, London (by
courtesy of John Haddon & Co). Right :* semi-silhouette individualised by a cleverly set rim high light. Light on the background. Phot : *Hugo van Wadenoyen, Cheltenham.*

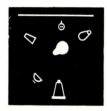

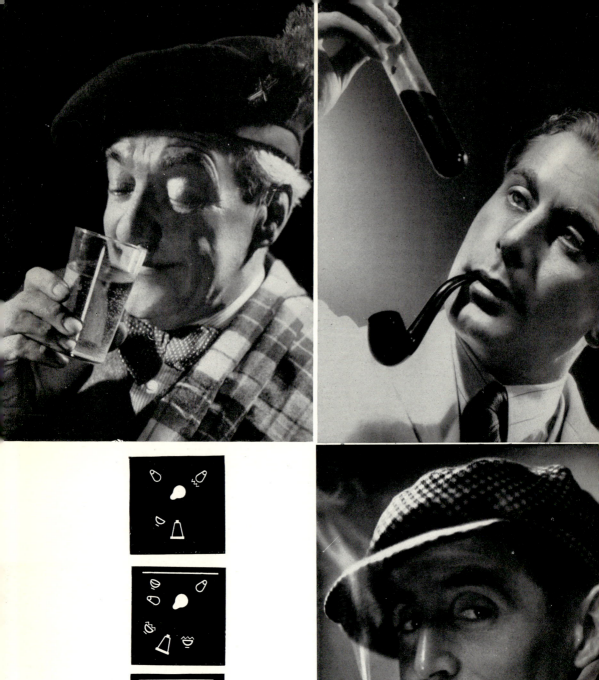

100

THE FULL FACE. *Top left :* cross-light produced by 45-degree spot lighting. First supplementary light : back-spot for hair definition : second supplementary light : frontal flood for shadow diffusion (omitted in diagram). *Top right :* Double rim-lighting. Basic light produced by two spots resulting in symmetrical light rim around the face. Supplementary light : frontal flood avoiding cast shadows.

Bottom : Central lighting. *Left :* normal central light. Basic light produced by slightly elevated flood causing small nose shadow. First supplementary light : background illumination. Second supplementary light produced by a flat reflector for shadow diffusion. *Centre :* Top-lighting. Basic light produced by strongly elevated flood. First supplementary light : background illumination. Second supplementary light : frontal flood. *Right :* Under-lighting. Basic light : directed to the face from a very low angle. Supplementary light by two spots symmetrically placed behind the model's head, achieving halo-effect.

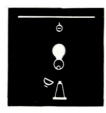

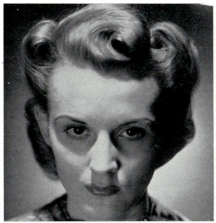

[0]

Portrait Barbara Stanwyck. Normal central lighting assisted by overhead lighting. Phot : *Hurrell, Hollywood.*
Opposite: The simplicity of a master photographer's lighting schemes, which achieve so much with so little, is again demonstrated. The basic lighting is a simple side light, supplemented by a frontal flood. Phot : *Hurrell, Hollywood.*

On page 104, *top left* : dramatic effect by underlighting. Phot :
H. von Perkhammer, Berlin. Top right : similar dramatic appearance
of unusually cast shadows achieved by top lighting. Phot : *Cyril
Arapoff, Oxford. Right* : Portrait Andre Simon. Double rim lighting, supplemented by flood from front and diffused flood on the
background. Phot : *W. Nurnberg, London (by courtesy of Mather &
Crowther).*

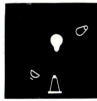

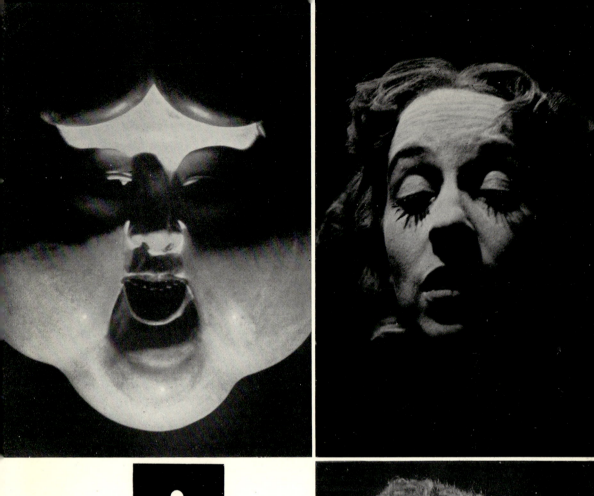

104

Third Supplementary Light: Only when backgrounds other than black are required; more or less flood on background to achieve grey tones.

Special Remarks: The pictorial effect of rim-lighting becomes more forceful when the background is darker in tone than the flood area of the face and becomes more subtle when the background tone is lighter than the flooded area of the face. The greatest luminosity in a rim-light picture is obviously always the main light produced by the basic illumination.

CROSS-LIGHT

This can be used for any kind of profile and, as we shall see later (see p. 107), also for three-quarter face and even full-face views. This particular light is called cross-light because a shadow is cast from the nose right across one side of the face in such a manner that this nose-shadow links up with the shadow of the cheek-bone. The light-and-shadow pattern thus created appears in the profile position as a rim light along the contours of the profile, at the same time producing a triangular light patch on the cheek facing the camera, and thus defining the line of cheek-bone.

In contrast to the four lighting treatments discussed above, this lighting aims at a three-dimensional effect by producing a very different pattern which defines the difference in perspective between front face and cheek. This lighting method is especially suitable for character work and men studies, but is not suited for use with a white background. Very deft and subtle effects can, however, be obtained if the shadows produced by the cross-lighting are lit up to approximately the same extent as the background; at the same time most masculine and powerful results are obtained by flooding the shadow parts of the face only slightly and using a black background.

Basic Light: Position similar to the one used for rim-lighting. Here, the lamp is moved slightly forward (away from the background) so that the light-beam catches the cheek facing the lens. Elevation of the lamp must be high enough to make the shadow of the nose long enough to link up with the shadow masses on the side of the face and to make the light patch on the cheek triangular in shape.

First Supplementary Light: Spot-light behind the head of sitter to produce rim-light effect on top and back of head.

Second Supplementary Light: Flood more or less diffused—beside the camera at an angle of 45° to the sitter's line of vision. The elevation of this flood should be such that it is just low enough to cast no nose-shadow.

Third Supplementary Light: For background either flat-lighting to achieve an even all-over tone, or an effect whereby the side of the background which is behind the face of the sitter is kept in a low key, gradually lightening to that side of the background which is behind the head of the sitter.

Special Remarks: I have suggested a spot-light as the light to be used for the basic light. My reason for this is that the whole idea of cross-lighting is based on a well-defined light-and-shadow pattern, and that a softening of the patterns

M 2

edges would contradict the meaning of the cross-light. If necessary, quite satisfactory results can be obtained with a parabolic reflector fitted with a projector bulb.

CENTRAL LIGHT

This type of light, when applied for full profile positions, aims at full illumination of the face, at the same time giving a very good rendering of the actual cheek-line by producing extensive plane and shadow at the side of the head. This light is usually used in connection with a black background and has no specific dramatic possibilities, but is very suitable for conventional portrait studies.

Basic Light: Flood (not diffused) placed in front of sitter's face, perhaps slightly towards the camera, elevation just high enough for the nose to cast a small shadow—which should not cover more than half of the upper lip.

Secondary Supplementary Light: diffused flood in an 45° angle position exactly as the one explained on p. 105.

Third Supplementary Light (Obligatory): Rim light for top and back of head, as explained before, or soft top lighting to pick up dark hair from a dark background.

Special Remarks: We shall see presently that this type of light is very useful for three-quarter face, and especially for full-face positions where the variations in the elevation of the basic light achieve astonishing effects. Its usefulness for full profile pictures will be found limited because too long shadows must be avoided.

THE THREE-QUARTER FACE

To simplify classification I include in the term "three-quarter face" all the intermediary stages which lie between profile and full-face, such as the three-quarter, half and quarter profile. It is only natural that, although each of these three positions may demand slight lighting adjustments, we have in principle always the same problems to solve. Three-quarter face positions are most frequently used in commercial portraiture. They offer the expressive possibilities of the full face but do not depend so much on either a classical profile contour or symmetrical features.

Obviously, a three-quarter face does not lend itself to the pure silhouette treatment, but, with this exception, the treatments already given for the profile are all suitable for three-quarter face lighting. It will be seen, however, that the lighting, although basically the same, is modified in details and consequently has a different rôle to play.

SEMI-SILHOUETTE

Most suitable for soft feminine glamour where a slickness combined with emotion is aimed at. When photographing three-quarter faces the semi-silhouette treatment should always be used with supplementary lighting in order to add the necessary sparkle and lightness. In order to give the relieving high-lights a chance, the tone of the background should be kept a light grey—not white. The tone of the sitter's face should be only slightly darker than the tone of the background.

Basic Light: Flood on background.
First Supplementary Light: Near to camera on the side facing the sitter. Elevation just high enough to avoid casting a nose shadow.
Second Supplementary Light: Spot-lighting from behind sitter so as to produce rim light on hair.
Third Supplementary Light (Obligatory): Spot-light producing rim light in such a position that it shines full on that side of the head (not the cheek) turned away from the camera. Make certain that, seen from the camera, this light gives a rim of light only along the cheek-bone and chin outline, but does not touch the nose; for a nose must be absolutely perfect if it is to be shown in a half-profile position accentuated by a rim light.
Special Remarks: A very effective method of treating the background in connection with half profile, and especially when subtle glamour effects are desired, is to create a halo of light around the head which quickly deteriorates towards its periphery. This *halo light can be achieved by placing a bare electric bulb behind the head of the sitter*, as near as possible to the background; another way of getting a similar but more contrasty effect is to project a halo of light on the background with a spot-light. If halo-lighting is used with a half-silhouette, the basic light will then be flat tone-lighting on the face and the halo will be composed around the subtly lighted form of the face.

CROSS-LIGHT

In three-quarter face positions the cross-light is most useful; it can be projected on either side of the face with much variety of effect. If you look at Rembrandt's paintings you will find that cross-light effects have been predominantly used; also note that Rembrandt usually has the typical light triangle on the far side of the sitter's face. To copy this method in photography is dangerous because it entails a lighting which flattens the perspective of the whole side of the face near the camera; it also tends to unbalance composition by making the face look unsymmetrical. I therefore advise the use of cross-lighting in such a way that the shadow side of the face faces the lens. The far side of the sitter's face becomes better balanced by the small light triangle. The extensive shadow area on the near side of the face can be balanced by creating a dark background behind the far side of the face.

Basic Light: Spot-light of the kind already explained. The actual position naturally depends on the position of the head and of the light triangle (near or far side of the face).
First Supplementary Light: Spot-light behind the head of sitter to produce rim-light effect on top and back of head. In male portraiture this supple-

mentary light can be slightly modified to obtain an interesting effect. If this spot-light, giving a rim on the back and top of the head, is moved very slightly away from the direction of the background, a rim of light can also be produced along the lower jaw. Care must be taken, however, not to break up the compact shadow masses intrinsic to the cross-light technique.

Second Supplementary Light: Flood, more or less diffused at an elevation which eliminates the casting of a nose shadow.

Special Remarks: I prefer to use cross-lighting for three-quarter faces on dark backgrounds, but this lighting can equally well be applied to any tone of background.

SIDE-LIGHT

I recommend the use of the side-light for three-quarter faces only, and not for the full-face position. The side-light is a compromise between the rim light and the cross-light. The position for the basic light source is consequently also between the one used for rim-lighting and the one used for cross-lighting. The effect aims at fully lighting the side of the face beyond the nose, leaving the other side—facing the camera—dark. Side-lighting is effective against dark backgrounds, and is most suitable for character studies of men. It demands a clever use of supplementary lighting.

Basic Light: Lamp position as explained above. Elevation—lamp at the height of top of sitter's head. The most suitable light source is a parabolic flood or diffused spot-light.

First Supplementary Light: Spot-light from back of sitter at a high elevation, throwing the ear-shadow downwards; the lamp must be moved just far enough forward (in the direction of the camera) for the side-face of the sitter to be vigorously lighted, thus creating texture and a very good definition of the cheek-bone and jaw line.

Second Supplementary Light: More or less diffused flood-lamp from the side of the camera facing the sitter.

Special Remarks: I wish to repeat again that this lighting is particularly masculine. Many other supplementary light positions can be found for this treatment, and certain modifications which, explained in detail, would lead too far.

CENTRAL LIGHT

Most applicable to half-profile positions. It has enormous possibilities for not only altering the character of the picture, but also for completely changing the look of the face itself. This is all the more amazing as central lighting is very straightforward. As its name implies, it always shines, more or less, "right in front of the sitter's nose". The amazing changes I have mentioned are obtained merely by altering the elevation of the lamp.

If the central light is brought high overhead, the forehead, nose, lower lip and cheek-bones give long and heavy shadows; thus high central lights are ideal for depression and headache pictures.

108

By shifting the basic lamp lower, we get the ordinary conventional kind of lighting—namely, that which produces a small shadow, more or less symmetrical, underneath the nose, with good definition of lips, eyes and cheeks. This kind of lighting is adequate if one wishes to keep the picture in a conventional mood.

By bringing the basic lamp still lower, until the nose shadow disappears, the face becomes very flat; lips, forehead, part of the face and the chin region are very badly defined. This third modification of the central light is really useful only when deliberately de-personalising a face. It gives some kind of ethereal quality to a half-profile when used in connection with light backgrounds and supplementary glamour lighting originating from behind the sitter.

The fourth modification of the central light is also called under-light. As the light source is placed under chin-level of the sitter, the face takes on a demoniac appearance. Usually one does not consciously perceive the visual effect of under-lighting, although we ought to be accustomed to it from the homely fireplace or the footlights of the stage, but it is a fact that every time one looks at a picture, especially a close-up picture, in which all shadows are cast upwards, one associates it with a somewhat Mephistophelian atmosphere.

Basic Light: This depends very much on the length and direction of the facial shadows. The reader can best compare methods of lamp-positioning and effects when looking at the pictures and diagrams. It is still better if he makes his own experiments. The basic light should normally be produced by a flood, but a spot-light can be substituted for it when very well-defined shadows are desired.

Supplementary Lights: Their main task here is to relieve the shadows and give extra definition to the top and the back of the sitter's head or, if so desired, give further illumination to the background. The main supplementary light—*i.e.*, the one relieving the depth of shadow—should always be placed on that side of the camera facing the sitter. The elevation of the lamp producing this light should always be low enough to avoid new shadows. Its sole purpose is to relieve existing shadows—not to create new ones.

THE FULL FACE

The full-face position in portraiture demands a good face. The human face seen absolutely from the front can, from the point of view of composition, be considered an extremely symmetrical form. If the natural symmetry of the face is disturbed by faults of the face itself, such as " spoon-ears " or " sword-noses ", this may be very interesting to the physiologist, or even to the photographic student, but I am sure the model to whom that face belongs will not be too pleased at having his shortcomings accentuated and memorised in a photograph. It is for this reason that, as mentioned before, three-quarter face positions (or at least positions which are just off the full-face angle) are usually employed in commercial portraiture.

Symmetrical lighting accentuates facial symmetry, and it is for this reason that all forms of central-lighting are predominantly employed for full-face positions. But cross-lighting can also find useful application. Besides these two there is a new method of lighting—the " double-rim light ".

CENTRAL LIGHT

Here, as in connection with half profiles, the central light gives to the photographer a wealth of latitude in the free moulding of form and in the infusion into his picture of a wide range of different sensorial qualities. Again it is the elevation of the light-source which brings forth the various pictorial and pyschological changes; it is in the full-face position that under-lighting can be most usefully employed.

Basic Light: For top lighting: light source as near as possible to lens of camera.—For normal position (*i.e.*, small nose shadow): approximately the same light position as above.—For extreme cases of top- and under-lighting: the light-source should be placed as near as possible either above the head or below the chin, thus creating the desired shadows without the lamp itself being in the field of camera-vision.

Supplementary Light: Produced by flood-lighting, diffused spherical reflectors being preferable. Position of supplementary light: one flood lamp on each side of camera somewhere half-way between camera and sitter, but not too near the sitter. It should be watched that these floods are not producing new shadows in the face, and it might for this reason be safer to substitute the two front lamps by paper reflectors which give a softer light.

Second Supplementary Light: It can be employed from right overhead, thus giving definition in the sitter's hair and creating a well-defined shoulder outline.

Special Remarks: It should be remembered that a central-light in connection with a full-face position has the important task of accentuating the symmetrical form of the face and of creating a symmetrical light-and-shadow pattern, though such rules must not be taken too literally. This symmetry of the face can be departed from by shifting the central light slightly out of the central axis if one has a good reason and justification for departing from the orthodox way of lighting.

DOUBLE-RIM LIGHT

The double-rim light is a special full-face lighting. We have already made its acquaintance without having called it by its proper name, *i.e.*, in the rim-lighting method applied to a profile picture where the light produced a second rim along the back of the head (see p. 92). I did not mention that this lighting had a double-rim light, because it was then merely a variation of the ordinary rim light which could be applied or not. Now, in the full-face position the double-rim light becomes a lighting scheme in itself. The reason for this is again the symmetry of the full face, which makes a one-sided rim-lighting appear out of balance. This double-rim light is the one exception where the basic light

110

is constructed by two lamp sources instead of one. The use of the double-rim light should be confined to slim faces; fat cheeks would be extraordinarily exaggerated by this type of lighting. It is ideal for glamour effects, and lends dramatic value to the picture when used in conjunction with a black background. It creates very subtle " pastel " effects when used with a light grey or light medium grey background. It is obvious that the double-rim light is a lighting method which never consists of a basic light alone. It always needs the addition of some kind of supplementary light.

Basic Light: Two spot-lights, one on each side slightly behind the sitter in a position which creates an outline on each side of the face without the light-beam touching the tip of the nose. Flood-lamps should not be employed, because they would shine too easily into the lens and lead to flare.

Supplementary Light: The most suitable supplementary light for this double-rim lighting is a completely frontal light; a diffused flood should for this reason be placed as near to the lens as possible, its elevation being low enough not to cast a nose shadow. This supplementary light can be modified if there should be any reason to do so, but any adjustment should be made by changing the elevation of the lamp, *i.e.*, shifting it perpendicularly rather than horizontally.

Special Remarks: The double rim-lighting can also be used as *supplementary effect* to other lighting schemes—especially in connection with central lighting (see p. 110).

CROSS-LIGHT

I think that one can say that the character of the cross-light contradicts the character intrinsic to the form created by a full-face position. At the same time, this divergence in character can very often be the means of achieving not only outstanding pictorial effects, but of conveying a certain restlessness or any unusual characteristics of the sitter. The use of cross-lighting in connection with a full-face position should therefore be strictly reserved for special purposes, and not be degraded by use without thought or purpose on every humdrum occasion.

Basic Light: The position of the lamps in relation to the face of the sitter has already been explained in detail. (See p. 105.)

Supplementary Light: Again the main supplementary light is one for lightening the shadows to any desired degree. The photographer must watch that this lamp produces no new shadow anywhere on the face. The best method of avoiding such lapses is to place a more or less diffused flood-lamp as near as possible to the line of camera-vision (*i.e.*, as near as possible to the lens), at an elevation which does not produce a shadow; the lamp should, however, be placed on the side of the lens facing the shadow side of the sitter's face.

LIGHTING A FIGURE

Lighting for figure work is nothing but an extension of that kind of lighting we already know from portraiture. It is therefore imperative that the

III

beginner should not attempt to tackle figure studies before he has mastered the lighting of a face. This is so much easier than the lighting of a figure, because each face presents about the same principal problems of lighting. A figure, on the other hand, requires a new and individual approach every time. While the head is a more or less static form, a figure changes its appearance most radically with every movement. Furthermore, a nude confronts us with an entirely different proposition from a dressed figure. To make matters even more complicated we have to decide if we are to photograph its full length or only a part of it. We cannot assess the number of different combinations of lighting, but we can form a few standard rules which form the basis to any attempt to successful figure lighting.

THE NUDE

The lighting of a figure in the nude can be treated from two distinctly different viewpoints.

We can aim either at creating a " graphic " high-key image or at an effect which is " typically photographic ", full of a three-dimensional character achieved by contrasting areas (not merely tones!) of light and shade.

The most popular method for high-key nudes seems to be " shadowless " lighting (see p. 79). The flattening effect of this lighting obviously appeals to those who consider a faithful reproduction of a bare body as an achievement and a dynamic shadow treatment as unwonted sensationalism. I am not going to discuss the " pros and cons " of the different schools, but I wish to state that shadowless photography applied to nudes demands the perfect body and the very definite intention to " glamourise " the body and make it less earthbound.

Those who prefer " realism " to " soap-box ideals ", and who wish to convey the warmth and expressiveness of the human body, will have to turn to other methods of lighting. They will have to include a certain amount of shadow in their picture to make the body live and give it its individuality. The building up of the lighting should be done as already explained, i.e., first the basic light has to be placed, and after this has been successfully done, the supplementary lighting must be built up.

Whenever we wish to stress the roundness and softness of a body the basic light source should be a flood. The elevation of the basic lamp should be such that it renders the anatomical structure of the body without exaggerating it. Shadows must therefore be placed so that they fall naturally, and consequently show the form of the body truly. After having achieved this object, we can then proceed to place our supplementary lighting, which can either be a rim high-light produced by a spot accentuating the various features of the body, or a flood diluting the shadows produced by the basic light—or both.

When photographing a nude " full-face ", we can also use the double-rim lighting, in which case the basic light is produced by two symmetrically placed spots. (See also p. 110.)

Nude profiles can be well treated as silhouettes or half-silhouettes.

112

MORE THAN THE HEAD ONLY. *Left :* Portrait Sir Adrian Boult. Low key effect achieved by cross lighting. Although face and hands form only a comparatively small area of the picture, the accent which they receive from the two spot lights gives them the emphasis of a large-scale close-up. Phot : *Howard Coster, London.*

Right : Portrait Arthur Wontner. Modified double rim light giving emphasis again mainly to the head and hands. Phot : *Howard Coster, London.*

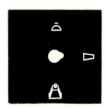

Portrait A. Kraszna-Krausz. Semi-silhouette with rim light effect both on profile and hands. Modified central light produced by baby spot. Phot : *Hugo van Wadenoyen, Cheltenham.*

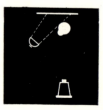

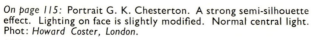

On page 115: Portrait G. K. Chesterton. A strong semi-silhouette effect. Lighting on face is slightly modified. Normal central light. Phot: *Howard Coster, London.*

114

FASHION PHOTOGRAPHY. *On page* 116 : the light effect on
the background, the high elevation of the basic central light and
the glamour shine on the hair achieved by a vigorous overhead
spot, create a preponderance of dark tones with carefully placed
high lights and a general impression of richness and warmth.
Phot : *W. Maywald, Paris.*

On page 117 : a brilliantly simple lighting scheme making use of
the reflecting properties of the book in the model's hands. Phot :
K. Schenker, London.

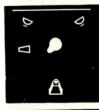

118

On page 118, *top left* : basic light : spot from the side rendering fur quality without touching the face. The first supplementary light source is a rim light on the opposite side of the figure. The second supplementary light is the halo on the background. Phot : *Gordon Coster, Chicago. Top right* : out-of-door imitation. Normal central light. Lack of supplementary lighting stresses the sunlight effect. Painted background flatly lit. Phot : *R. Owen, Chicago. Right* : basic lighting is the background light. The first supplementary light is a frontal flood, producing an almost shadowless effect on the face. The second supplementary light is supplied by a strong spot light from side face behind the model, giving a well-placed rim effect both on the face and horse, and at the same time relief and texture to the black areas. Phot : *C. Conrad, New York.*

On page 119 : a dance study of strongly emotional character. Basic effect produced by elevated and modified rim lighting and supplemented by a further rim light on the lower part of the figure. Phot : *F. S. Lincoln, New York.*

Portrait Claire Dodd. A paradoxical lighting scheme. The upper part of the figure is treated with a normal central light, while the lower part is lit from behind. A somewhat unreal but intriguing " movie " effect is the result. Phot : *Hurrell, Hollywood.*

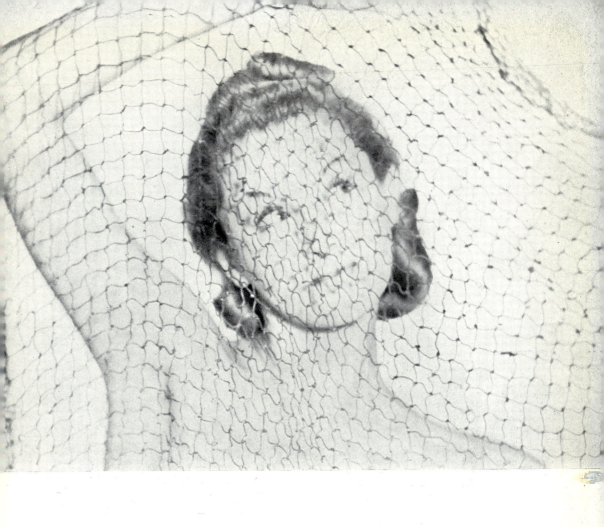

LIGHTING THE NUDE.   High key : dead frontal lighting to eliminate shadows and three-dimensional body effect is a popular treatment for nudes. It kills realism and achieves etheric quality. In the case of our example, the net in the foreground, doubled in its effect by the faint shadows, serves as an additional means of creating an artificial appearance. Phot : *Jan de Meyere, Stockholm.*

121

Left : nude in dramatic style. A single spot light gives the figure a somewhat hard, sculpture-like appearance. Phot : *Edwin Smith, London.*

Opposite : nude with body emphasis. Semi-silhouette effect relieved by rim light and top light. Modelling and warmth have not been sacrificed, and crudeness yet avoided. Phot : *U. Lang-Kurz, Stuttgart.*

On page 124 : the symmetrical character of the double rim lighting stresses the quiet atmosphere and the symmetry of composition. Phot : *W. Nurnberg, London (by courtesy of J. Tate & Partners).*

GROUPS. *On page* 125 : An unusual amount of lighting and spot lights from various angles have been used for this picture. This effort was necessary to create exposure conditions (1/100 at *f* 11) for a candid shot. Phot : *W. Nurnberg, London.*

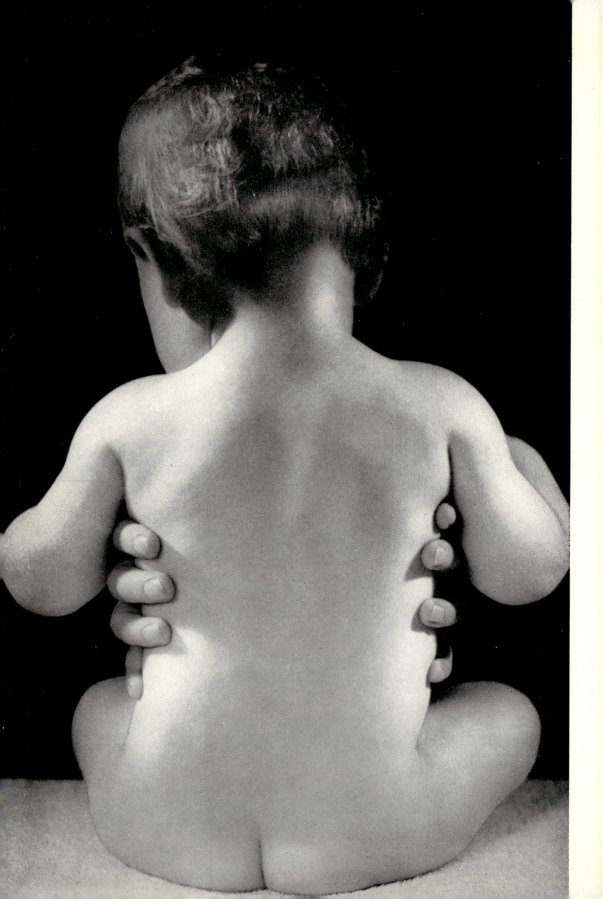

Left : the front figures are lit by separate units, The rim effects on each of them are produced by the two basic light sources, while the background figure gets its illumination by the general flood and overhead lighting only. Phot : *K. Schenker, London.*

Right : an under-angle shot of strong diagonal composition emphasised by rim lighting on man's head and arm. The girl is lit individually by cross lighting method and a separate hair light from the back. The paper in the foreground is also lit separately by diffused flood, assisted by a second flood for general lighting of the whole subject. Phot : *W. Nurnberg (by courtesy of J. Haddon & Co., Ltd.).*

HANDS AND FEET. *Opposite :* simplest possible treatment for lighting a hand. Phot : *Ifor Thomas, London.*
On page 128, top left : basic light produced by a top-angle spot, supplemented by very diffused front lighting. Phot : *Sougez, Paris. Top right :* the hands lit by two spot lights of great intensity to get short exposure times. Phot : *W. Nurnberg, London (by courtesy of John Tate & Partners). Right :* simple modelling by a complicated light scheme. Phot : *W. Nurnberg, London.*

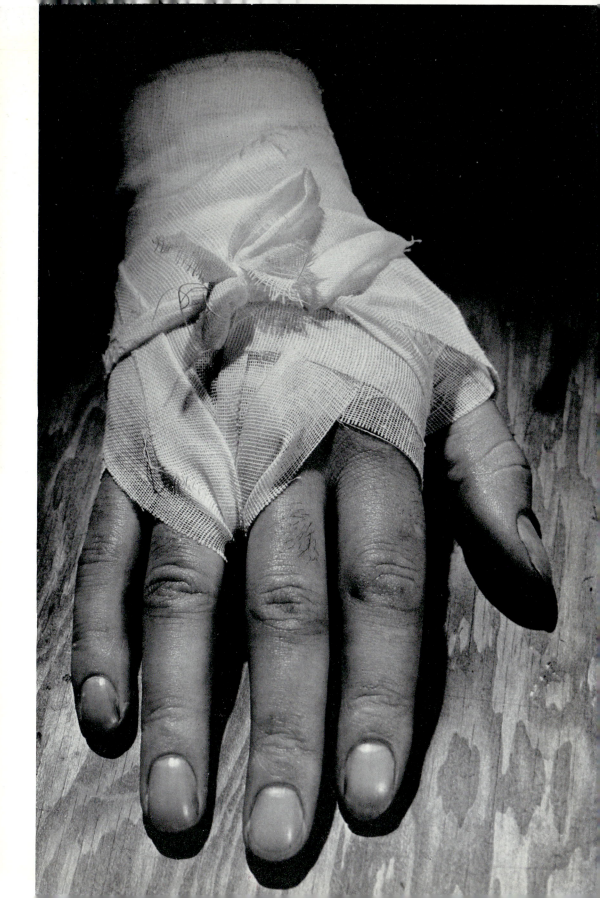

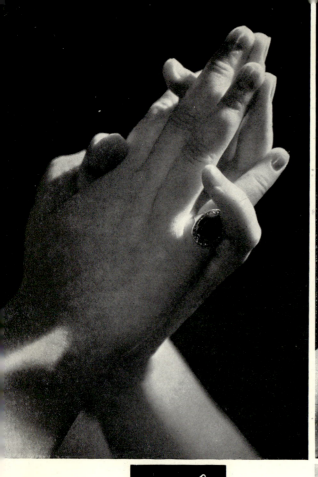

128

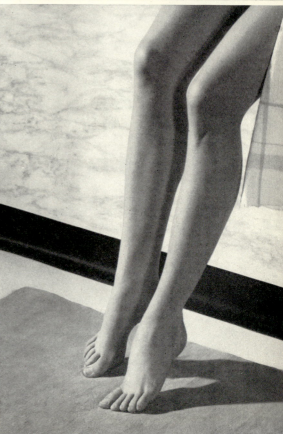

The dressed figure gives us again different problems. The main reason for this is that, nine times out of ten, we photograph dressed figures for advertising or other utilitarian purposes which govern the application of lighting. These purposes are so manifold that the kinds of lighting to be employed vary greatly. The lighting for a fashion picture must naturally be different from that for a " straight " commercial figure study. Here are a few practical hints.

First of all we must know that shadowless photography is not to be applied for dressed figures. Flat lighting is most unsuitable to show detail and texture. It also does not render adequately the form of a body which is hidden but at the same time accentuated by a dress. In order to convey the attitude of a figure clearly, we have to employ *angle-lighting, which dissects the image into definite areas of varying tones, and thus gives modelling to the figure.*

When photographing a figure slightly sideways, the side should be kept darker than the front; otherwise we not only get a flat and shapeless image, but also render the figure much too wide.

A figure photographed from the front (which should be posed not rigidly but in a soft elongated S shape) should be lit by a kind of cross-lighting or rim or even double-rim lighting so as to accentuate the curves and, consequently, the action of the body.

The building up of figure-lighting can now be done in two principal ways. Firstly, we can light the head and shoulders, and then add the lighting necessary for the body, or *vice versa.* This first way will usually be employed by the amateur who does not possess lamps which emit a light-beam of a width sufficient to cover an upright standing figure, or to illuminate the total extent of the figure. The second way—open to the professional—is to employ light sources big enough to create a basic light for the whole of the figure (including head and shoulders). But even he will find it often useful to *light the head separately from the body;* this applies especially when he has to deal with a dark garment which needs a much longer exposure time than the face, or whenever he may wish to render the face and bare shoulders as a semi-silhouette while the garment is presented in full and plastic light. These considerations play an important part in fashion photography. While some differentiation of lighting for face and figure is quite permissible, an excessive and unnatural differentiation, tending to divide the picture into two separately lit components, should be avoided.

Another important problem in connection with figure photography is the lighting of the background. When dealing with a realistic setting, such as the wall of a room, the lighting scheme will be obvious. Kitchen or " sunny-room " backgrounds need " general flood "; but " evening interiors " or gruesome cellar surroundings call for subdued and eerie effects which are usually obtained by angle spot-lighting or cast shadow effects on the background.

The issue becomes more involved if we choose a plain background on which to " paint " an abstract light-and-shadow pattern in order to create a certain

P

129

atmosphere. Here the lighting of the background element becomes just as important as the lighting on the figure itself. The background takes on a life of its own, a life which must supplement the realism of the foreground with an abstract quality. This kind of background lighting depends firstly on tones and secondly on shapes. The shapes are determined by the kind of lamp and the angle of light incidence (here our knowledge of the bogus shadow comes in most handy see p. 75). The tone is determined by supplementary lighting which controls the extent of dilution of the dark areas.

Whatever kind of background treatment we wish to apply to figures, it is essential that we keep the figure well away from the background. An exception to the rule is permitted on those occasions where the pictorial theme demands a cast and annexed shadow from the object on the background.

HINTS ON THE LIGHTING OF GROUPS

We have to distinguish between Portrait-Groups (head and shoulders) and Figure-Groups. The required lighting is, in principle, the same as for single head-studies or single figure-studies. There are, however, a few additional lighting problems which must be investigated.

We first must realise that *a group is one unit*. From this it follows that the lighting must be such that the unity of the pictorial composition is not disturbed by disconnected and sporadic patches of light and shadow. In other words, the lighting must connect the individual models with each other—not separate them! In order to achieve this, the scheme of lighting must be preconceived and not arrived at haphazardly.

When dealing with *large* figure-groups (those showing three persons or more, often found in advertisements) our best approach is to use as *basic light a large general flood*, which covers the whole of the group as evenly as possible. It is then left to the supplementary spot-lighting to accentuate details and to individualise carefully the various units according to a plan based on the story of the picture.

The exact character of the supplementary lighting depends largely on our intentions. Figures or faces which are lighted by cross-lighting, for instance, will be more conspicuous than those given a normal central lighting. In this way we can emphasise a figure in the background by giving it a type of light demanding more attention than that used on the more dominating foreground figures. We can obviously reverse this example and subdue a figure in the background still further, either by rendering it darker or by giving a more interesting play of light and shadow on the foreground units. I wish to repeat here that the accentuation by lighting must on no account be overdone, because we shall otherwise obtain just those patchy effects which must in all circumstances be avoided. Always bear in mind that the accentuating, supplementary lighting on the individual figures must conform with their individual characters. It will not do to light a male figure with a glamorous double-rim

130

lighting while its female counterpart is treated with a masculine cross-light effect.

If the different units of a group are more or less on the same optical level we can often achieve plastic modelling by using only one single supplementary light source producing a "sunny" high-light effect. The simpler the lighting the more will it help to create a homogeneous image and convey the feeling of perfect harmony between the individual units of the picture.

These rules become more significant when applied to portrait-groups, as they aim primarily at "characterisation". (The purpose of figure-groups is usually restricted to the representation of a certain setting.) Let us therefore remember that, if the purpose of a group picture is to demonstrate *similarity* of character, all units of that group should be lighted by the *same type* of supplementary lighting (not necessarily by only one light source). If, on the other hand, the aim is to demonstrate *differences* of character or to emphasise one unit in relation to another, each unit should be given its own appropriate lighting.

For portrait-groups the lighting should be built up in the orthodox way, *i.e.*, *not* by starting with a general flood, but by determining and carefully placing the basic light effects. The fact that in portrait-groups the different units are usually very near to each other makes it imperative to construct the lighting scheme systematically and accurately, or the result will be a maze of cast shadows.

THE LIGHTING OF HANDS

The lighting of hands depends to a great extent on the movement and individual position of the hand, and it is therefore difficult to set up rules which would cover this particular branch of photography systematically. There is hardly another field requiring more personal experience and open-mindedness from the photographer. One must not cling too tightly to preconceived ideas. At the same time, there are a number of rules which are generally applicable.

First we have to consider if we have to photograph an outstretched hand or a fist. The shallow form of an *outstretched hand demands a soft basic lighting* which—supplemented with a few carefully placed high-lights—gives good modelling. A *fist calls for a contrasty spot-lighting* which dissects the form of the hand into distinct areas of light and shadow and which makes the bend of the fingers and the typical three-dimensional character of the fist clearly perceptible.

We then have to take into account whether the hands are closely connected with a background—consequently casting annexed shadows—or whether they are detached from the background so that the background shadows can be isolated and shifted outside the field of camera-vision.

It is obvious that hands which are far away from a background can be lighted much more effectively than those near a background. The proximity of a

131

background—being nearly always in the way of the lamps—makes, indeed, many light variations impossible. One of the most dramatic and appropriate methods of lighting for an outstretched hand is, for instance, the double-rim light (see p. 110); but, as we have seen in the portrait section, this particular lighting is based on an acute angle of light incidence, only to be achieved by having the object well away from the background.

You will find that you have to be most careful in the choice of the camera-angle in order to avoid optical distortions (especially watch bent fingers, which tend to be easily foreshortened). Inappropriate lighting will emphasise these distortions. For instance: if you light a hand in front of a black background in such a way that the foreshortened link of a finger is in " shadow ", then the distortion will be stressed. This, however, does *not* imply that distortions should be rectified by playing about with the lighting; to rectify these faults we have to go back to their source, *i.e.*, alter the position of either the hand or the camera.

Another fact determining the choice of lighting is the object of the picture. Hands of men—especially in connection with industrial work or any other kind of manual labour—should be treated with vigorous spot-light effects which stress the exertion of power and energy. Women's hands obviously demand an entirely different treatment. Here the image must be glamorous and uncomplicated, and it follows that flood-lighting will play a more prominent part.

LIGHT AND SHADOW APPLIED TO THE INANIMATE

Under the heading of this chapter falls everything usually described as still-life Photography or " Reproduction ". These two terms cover the photography of everything from flat originals to the most intricate groupings of three-dimensional matter. My object here is to investigate the problems of still-life photography from the lighting viewpoint only.

We have to tackle this wide field systematically, and must therefore first draft a plan of campaign. The first and simplest step is the reproduction of flat originals; next, the reproduction of surfaces which are light-absorbent; thirdly, the reproduction of predominantly reflecting surfaces.

THE REPRODUCTION OF FLAT ORIGINALS

Some professional photographers do nothing but reproduce flat originals, such as black-and-white drawings, oil paintings, etc. Also belonging to this class of work is the reproduction of fabrics in the flat, as used for catalogue illustrations. The beginner very often tends to under-estimate the difficulties connected with this " straightforward " photographic process.

The problems of lighting of this kind of work can roughly be summed up in one sentence: *The light sources must be placed so that they illuminate the surface evenly and completely, and so that the material being photographed does not produce concentrated reflections.*

Firms specialising in photographic reproduction work have often to use a variety of intricate apparatus, for they have not only to produce an image which is evenly lighted, but one which reproduces colours in tone values which have either to correspond with the colours of the original, or are purposely faked. The professional photographer very often uses discharge lamps for reproduction purposes and has also all the necessary filters at his disposal. The amateur will obtain good results with the help of the following suggestions:

(1) Use as light sources spherical reflectors and frosted bulbs only.

(2) Never put lamps in such a position that the incident light meets the

surface perpendicularly, in other words, place them sideways. Also note that it is imperative that each lamp produces a light of the same efficiency, and that they are placed at the same distance from *and* absolutely symmetrically about the flat surface to be reproduced.

(3) For not too large areas two flood-lamps are adequate. For larger propositions four flood-lights may be required.

(4) In conjunction with tungsten filament light the amateur will find a set of filters necessary; deep yellow, dark orange, medium red and green will usually cover his requirements.

RENDERING TEXTURES

Texture rendering is essentially a matter of lighting. Even if we admit the importance of other considerations, such as camera-technique and the object-arrangement, we cannot get round the fact that the rendering of textures stands or falls by the right application of light. We shall be more successful in our aim if the surface to be photographed does not reflect light excessively. Needless to say, we cannot pick up texture where there is none, as in transparent or purely reflective surfaces, but neither must we assume that a light-absorbing surface always lends itself easily to texture rendering. We have seen, for instance (p. 19), that black velvet absorbs approximately 99·7% of the incident light—yet it is almost impossible to represent black velvet successfully by means of photography.

We want a surface which is rough enough to become, under the influence of light, a pattern of minute highlight and shadow particles. It is obvious that *the shallower are the " bumps " constituting the texture of the surface, the more oblique must be the angle of incident light.* Furthermore, it is obvious that *the harder the light, the more pronounced will be the surface-impression of light and shadow;* the reason being the perfected definition of the shadow parts.

FABRICS

Let us first clear up one point which is very often misunderstood. I have found that if one whispers into the ear of the student the word " fabric " it seems to act like magic. You see him smile and exclaim, " Another chance to pick up texture ". I certainly like enthusiasm, but in recent years the business of the rendering of fabric texture has been grossly exaggerated. After all, texture is not everything which counts in a fabric and which is characteristic of it. Pattern, for example, has very often been neglected in " modern " photography; especially when woven, it is often sacrificed to the forcing of texture and thereby lost completely.

Fabric photography is not " Art ", nor is it usually done merely for fun; mostly it is produced for advertising purposes—for the purpose of selling goods. Therefore the photographer has no right to exaggerate texture in a photographic image when the fabric does not demand it. On the other hand, photo-
134

graphers who have not the ability to make good texture photographs should not excuse their failing by saying that they were reproducing some insignificant pattern when the fabric demanded a bold texture treatment.

It has been already mentioned (p. 134) that the more one wishes to force a texture the more oblique must be the angle at which the light falls upon the surface, and that the extent of light diffusion determines the extent of texture rendering. If we could look upon the rendering of a fabric's surface as the only task of a fabric photograph, things would be easy. Having a piece of fabric lying on a table, and placing the carbon spot-light nearly as low as the height of the table, so that the light-beam just touches the fabric on the table, we shall observe (especially if we view this " scene " more or less against the light) that we obtain a tremendous roughness—probably an exaggerated roughness. We could then try to amend this basic lighting by using a very diffused flood to soften the contrast. Or we can choose another way—by elevating the basic light source to produce shorter-texture shadows, and thus a less exaggerated effect. As a third alternative, we can use for our basic light source, not a carbon spot-light, but a light of softer quality, e.g., a diffused filament spot-light, or even a screened parabolic flood.

Apparently, taking a certain amount of logical thinking for granted, texture rendering as such is not so difficult. But something more is needed. Most fabrics have a certain " touch " about them, and they must therefore not be set plainly on a table, but must rest loosely and in an unsymmetric but graceful fold pattern. This naturally confronts the photographer with new problems, because a low placing of his light will now produce big patches of shadow— shadow in which there is no drawing. The proper way to light a loosely draped fabric is to *place one's basic light source in such a way that it gives a rim light which accentuates rough outline pattern constructed by the fabric's natural folds.* This basic light must be retained as the strongest light and must domi- nate the whole lighting scheme. *The second light is a supplementary light which aims at picking up texture without overpowering the basic light.* Often it will be found that, here and there, shadows are still too dark, and that one must therefore employ *a third lamp (usually a diffused flood) which gives just enough relief to the shadow parts in question.*

Different types of fabrics obviously demand different kinds of treatment:

A ROUGH TWEED requires low angle lighting picking up the hairiness and roughness of the material. Tweeds therefore should be treated with hard low-angle lighting for the basic light.

SILK wants softness, glamour and sheen. We should therefore use a flood directly thrown on to it so as to create reflection which then should be supplemented by a vigorous spot-light effect (produced by a filament spot) in order to accentuate pattern and give " depth " to the image.

DAMASK should be treated in a purely reproductive manner because its main merit is the difference of tone created by a woven pattern. The same applies to any other fabrics (e.g., chintzes, etc.) the sole pictorial merit of which is their pattern. It will be found that, in order to render a damask pattern successfully, the use of a contrast filter is desirable.

The material which demands the treatment most similar to that of fabrics is leather, especially the matt-surfaced varieties such as suede. The principal difference between lighting leather and lighting fabrics is that leather is usually photographed in the finished article, while fabrics are mostly photographed in bulk; it follows that when photographing leather we have to deal with a material which has a more or less flat surface and does not lend itself to draping.

Needless to say, leather does not give the photographer the same chance of creating " atmosphere " as do fabrics. However, one should not assume that a good pictorial effect cannot be created out of leather goods. As we cannot expect too much help from the arrangement of the material itself, the perfect rendering of texture becomes all the more important, and all effects have therefore to be created by the interplay of light and shadow.

SUEDE LEATHER. The photographer has to distinguish between rough suede and smooth suede. Smooth suede is obviously a much more tricky subject. Its texture is so fine that it is difficult to " get hold of it " with lighting. Before one starts actually to build up one's lighting on a suede-leather object one must brush the surface so that all the " hairs " run in one direction—otherwise it will look patchy, an effect emphasised under strong light.

Suede, having a very " low texture " surface, demands a *lighting which meets it at an exceedingly oblique angle. For the basic light source carbon-arc lighting is the best.*

It is somewhat difficult to indicate the actual positions of the lamps, as these depend on the type of object, on the kind of suede-leather surface and on which way it has been brushed. It is therefore best to be open-minded and consider each individual problem as it comes. But when experimenting, *one must always view the object from the point at which the camera sees it, and from no other.* Especially when dealing with very fine textures and surfaces which produce a concentrated reflection, the smallest divergence of viewpoint makes all the difference.

With *black suede leather* one must realise that one has to create a grey-toned image because —obviously—a black surface can never show any texture at all. It will help, therefore, to surround it with a background which consists—at least to a certain extent—of deep black which will help to render tones of the suede leather to better advantage. The point is that black suede leather has a very low coefficient of reflection, while a white or light grey background would reflect a very considerable amount of light. We would require a considerable length of exposure time in order to get a satisfactory image of the suede surface; an exposure time which will naturally be far too long for the light background. By using a background of, let us say, a middle-grey tone, it becomes, under the influence of the long exposure, a lighter grey and at the same time the black suede surface will be correctly rendered.

HOGSKIN. Hogskin has certain photographic similarities to suede. Again the photographer has to distinguish between two kinds—rough matt and slightly glazed. (I am sure that leather experts will be deeply disgusted with this unorthodox classification. I hope they will excuse it, because I am looking at materials from a purely photographic point of view and am classifying them accordingly.)

The rough variety can be given carbon spot-lighting, meeting the surface at an oblique angle, and preferably shining towards the camera position. Diffused flood-lighting should be employed to control any excessive rendering of texture.

The glazed variety of hogskin demands a different treatment. The surface, being slightly glossy, not only reflects light, but also produces diffused reflections. The lighting should be so built that *the first lamp creates some kind of light-and-shadow pattern* which demonstrates the shape of the object—without actually rendering the texture of the object itself to any great extent. *The texture is now stressed by the supplementary light, a very diffused flood* usually being the most suitable. In certain circumstances a *second supplementary light will be necessary*

136

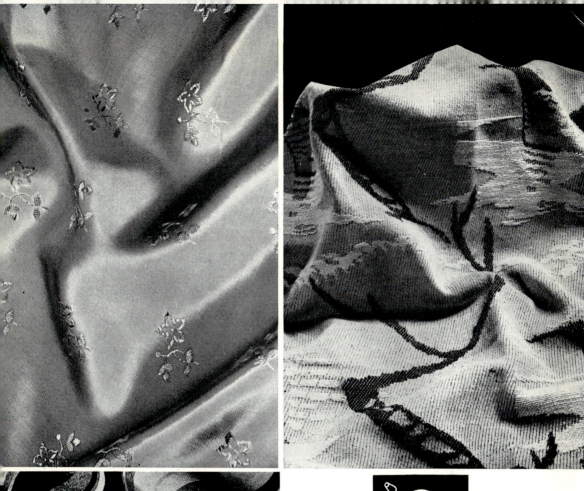

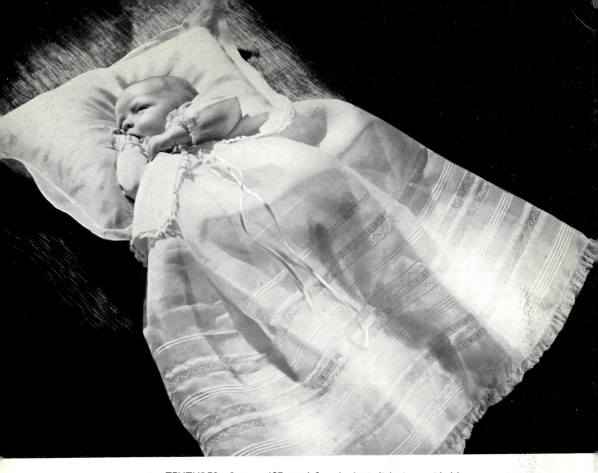

TEXTURES. *On page* 137, *top left :* the basic light is provided by a spot stressing fold pattern and sheen. Supplementary flood illuminates the large shadow areas, but it is carefully placed to retain sufficient depth in the folds. Phot : *W. Nurnberg (by courtesy of Harvey Nichols Ltd.). Top right :* furnishing fabric in bold light and shadow treatment. Basic lighting supplied by a spot giving pattern and rendering texture. Supplementary light, diffused frontal flood. Phot : *W. Nurnberg, London (by courtesy of The Studio Ltd.). Left :* flood lighting but a very appropriate one for rendering pattern. Phot : *H. Gorny, New York.*

A delightful baby study. The basic lighting is produced by a spot which gives to the picture its feeling of texture and warmth. Phot : *Doric Studio, London.*

Opposite : the lighting of this picture consists of two parts. Firstly, a normal 45° angle lighting against the camera, supplemented by a flood, and dealing exclusively with chair and cat. Secondly, a low angle spot to give a fireside effect and an added feeling of warmth, homeliness and comfort. The deep texture picked up by the supplementary light underlines this tendency. Phot : *W. Nurnberg, London (by courtesy of Lovell, Rupert & Curtis Ltd.).*

139

The opposite of rendering textures. A pure silhouette treatment giving intriguing pattern effect. Phot : *F. S. Lincoln, New York.*

LEATHER. *Left* : hogskin handbag. The " tooth and sheen" of the leather could be captured only by the combination of hard and soft lighting from various angles, which was achieved by the use of a carbon arc and an incandescent spot. Phot : W. Nurnberg, London (by courtesy of Colman Prentice).

Right : black suede handbag lit by carbon arc spot for basic lighting. An incandescent spot placed slightly underneath the table level gives depth to the bag without interfering with the background. Phot : W. Nurnberg, London (by courtesy of Colman Prentice).

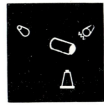

PAPER. The treatment is a good example of spot lighting and what it can do. The predominance of the shadows gives a difficult material an almost sensorial quality. Phot : *W. G. Briggs, London.*

FLOWERS. Combination of direct rim lighting and purely reflected (indirect) '' body '' lighting. The limited use of the vigorous direct light on the edges of the flower and the unusual number of subtle tones in the centre give this flower picture considerable charm. Phot : *I. von Kuhnsberg, Danzig.*
Vigorous high lights give the flower its lightness. The hardness of the light is controlled so as not to lose texture and drawing. The shadows have been carefully diluted by the supplementary flood. Phot : *E. Landau, Paris.*

On page 144 : the lighting is aimed more to give emphasis to a geometrical composition pattern than to render texture. Phot : *H. Gorny, New York.*

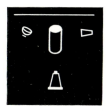

to "*draw*" *in a few final highlight effects;* this should, however, be applied as sparingly as possible, so as not to make the leather surface look stony. The reader will have guessed by now that the second supplementary light thus described demands a *spot-light* of not too high an intensity.

CROCODILE. Again we are confronted with a fresh problem, and again must differentiate. Firstly, we have to deal with that kind of skin surface which is highly glossy, comparatively flat and intersected by a number of irregular lines. Especially when polished, it gives off very strong, and sometimes even concentrated, reflections. The second kind has a very horny and plastic surface moulding which catches light beautifully and produces substantial shadow forms.

We shall see in practice that crocodile always shows a certain amount of smooth surface which reflects. Our *basic light* should be a *spot*, and again aim at *determining light and shadow on the background and the shape of the object*, while the *supplementary light* has the task of *rendering the leather surface* in a typical manner. Again, a diffused flood is used for the supplementary lighting.

The amount of reflection to be produced on the surface depends not only on the grade of polish, but also on the requirements dictated by the photographer's client. Sometimes only very *soft reflections* are wanted, and in this case the supplementary light source will be a *paper-reflector* instead of a lamp.

LIZARD- AND SNAKE-SKINS. What interests us in lizard- and snake-skins is not so much texture as pattern and the obvious treatment indicated is one of " reproduction ". Besides reproducing the shape of the object into which the skin has been manufactured, the photographer has to capture all the beautiful irregularities of the natural markings.

As we usually have to deal with three-dimensional objects, not the flat skin, adherence to the orthodox reproduction technique is not essential. We can therefore employ either spot- or flood-lighting from any angle which may seem appropriate as long as we take care that our lamps are so placed in relation to object and camera that we *do not obtain reflections which* " *fog* " *the leather surface* and thus eliminate the pattern impression.

SMOOTH CALF AND SIMILAR LEATHERS. In these smooth leathers—most commonly used for handbags, etc.—we have a perfect combination of " tooth and sheen "; it is here that the photographer has great scope to prove his skill in leather lighting. He can roughen or smooth the surface at will; *the more angle spot-lighting used the more toothy will the surface be*, while a soft and reflected lighting makes the surface smoother. The best solution is found, as usual, by combining both treatments without exaggerating either.

Before producing reflections on these kinds of leathers the shape and form of the object and the texture of the surface must first be properly rendered. The reflections should never be harsh and the best results are obtained by keeping them properly controlled.

PAPER

Paper, with its great variety of texture and quality, and the fact that it is sometimes semi-transparent while on other occasions it presents itself as an opaque substance full of " body ", confronts the photographer with a number of problems.

One must keep in mind that it is the job of the photographer to convey through an image the characteristics of the object. With semi-transparent papers the lighting has thus to render this characteristic, and should be such that no undue reflections are created to make the surface look " milky " or opaque.

In the case of opaque paper structures the photographer can light his subject in three ways: (1) In a manner which is appropriate to the familiar interpretation of paper in use; (2) To reproduce pattern by means of a flat reproduc-

R

tion technique; (3) To render texture by means of exceedingly oblique angle lighting and close-up treatment which create an image exaggerating the natural structure of the paper's surface.

Treatment I is usually applied to writing-paper, newspapers, magazines—in short, to all those papers where character is of only secondary importance, but where the range of its usefulness has primarily to be illustrated. Treatment 2 would be applied for printed wallpapers and decorative packing papers, etc., treatment 3 for heavy and rough paper surfaces such as embossed wallpapers and Lincrustas, the effectiveness of which relies on texture, or for corrugated papers, rough packing-papers and such like.

Opaque paper substances should be treated in much the same way as leather or fabric, and the student, having mastered the rendering of those two materials, will find no special difficulties when photographing paper.

FLOWERS

Flowers are delicate things. Perhaps it is wrong to classify them under the title "inanimate", but, seen photographically, they do present the same problem as does still-life.

Here is one rule which should always be observed: the texture must never be exaggerated, but rendered in such a way that it does not differ from that impression perceived by the human eye in normal circumstances. Shadows should not be over-heavy, and the photographer should try to put in as many subtle half-tones as his subject is able to carry.

Soft lighting should therefore be used for the basic illumination. Hard lighting easily results in "chalky" effects and in a loss of modelling. When photographing flowers indoors we can either use artificial lighting only or artificial lighting mixed with daylight. But always it will be necessary to employ at least two light sources, one for the basic and the other (or others) for the supplementary effects.

The exact position of the light sources depends, of course, on the shape and type of the flower, and it will therefore vary accordingly. In principle, however, there are two main methods of basic lighting. Firstly, we have a *slightly elevated backlighting* giving rim light on the sides and on top of the object. These "against-the-light" shots render the shape of a flower beautifully and convey the whole delicacy of translucent blossom. It is necessary to supplement the basic light with a soft flood effect which brings drawing into the shadows and also avoids "heaviness". The second lighting method is a *side-lighting*, which, being supplemented by a flood, gives good form rendering especially when applied to non-translucent plants (cacti, etc.).

In both instances the basic light can be supplied either by a flood or a *diffused* spot or by the sun, the supplementary lighting by diffused daylight, diffused flood, white paper reflectors, silver paper reflectors or mirrors.

Artificial-light sources must *never be placed too near the flowers*, for they are easily affected by excessive heat. If absolutely essential, one can strengthen a

146

flower by threading a piece of thin wire into its stem. At the same time a strong illumination is desirable, because some flowers turn towards the light very quickly, and only by short exposure-times can we avoid moved images.

Another important factor in flower photography is the treatment of backgrounds. A common mistake is to produce a background element which overpowers, through its realism, the delicate structure of the flower. What a chance has a flower photographer to infuse his picture with atmosphere, just by painting his background with soft light and shadow effects! Altering the tone of the background is one of the means by which the character of the object or its significance can be emphasised.

REFLECTING SURFACES

The task confronting the photographer in the photography of textures is an obvious one: to create an image which illustrates the structure as well as the " character " of the texture. But when photographing reflecting and semi-reflecting surfaces his task is not so clear, because, although being reflecting to varying degrees, some of them must be treated in a way which conceals their reflectant faculty. This applies especially to polished wood. On the other hand, we have reflecting surfaces the successful rendering of which depends solely on the rendering of just this faculty for reflection which we have to suppress in other cases.

REFLECTIONS AND CATCHLIGHTS

The danger of a powerful reflection producing a flare and halation is one against which one must always be on guard. Since a softening of the reflection will often destroy the texture and character of the material, it may be better to weaken the principal light source rather than diffuse it.

Where reflections have to be entirely suppressed—for instance, in photographing glazed pictures—or where a reproduction is required of, say, the patterning of a china ornament without any attempt at plasticity or modelling, a *Pola-screen is very valuable.*

This is a type of filter which depends upon a totally different principle from those so far considered (p. 15). To understand the action of the Pola-screen, we have to realise that normally, light vibrates in all directions. Light is, however, said to be *polarised* when it vibrates in one plane only. When ordinary light is specularly reflected from a smooth non-metallic surface it becomes polarised; consequently, by filtering out light which is polarised in that particular plane, and passing only unpolarised light, we can reduce the reflection or glare from a shiny object, permitting the texture to be seen by diffuse reflection.

Polaroid consists of microscopic crystals, having the power of polarising light by transmission, which are embedded and correctly orientated in a transparent substance. A Pola-screen consists of a layer of this material, cemented between glasses, and so mounted that it can be rotated to bring the plane of polarisation in the direction desired, which is best found by viewing the image on the focusing screen, or by holding the filter over the view-finder, and then mounting it on the lens at the same angle.

Polaroid has a considerable neutral density, and necessitates an increase of exposure of four or five times, although developments are taking place which may result in the production of a more transparent material.

But although in theory it is possible to rotate the Pola-screen to produce any desired suppression of reflections, in practice this may have the effect of accentuating unwanted reflections. For this reason, Pola-screens are more often used in outdoor photography, where the light source cannot be controlled to any extent, than in the studio.

Where any extensive area of specular reflection appears, some object will naturally be imaged as a catchlight. Not only should this object be appropriate to the subject—one would, for instance, not dream of imaging a factory window in the reflections of expensive silverware—but it must be regarded as part of the picture. Its lines must enhance, and not detract from, the modelling of the surface.

In order to bring a certain kind of system into the investigation I shall start with those materials which demand a total or partial suppression of reflection, and then pass on in degrees to those in which the rendering of reflection is all-important.

WOOD

Wood (like leather) is usually photographed as an article of merchandise, and not in the piece. The lighting of a wooden object has to achieve two ends. First, to reproduce as perfectly as possible the grain of the wood; secondly, to render the object itself in a plastic and attractive way. This twofold purpose must always be kept in mind, because a lighting which renders the grain successfully but fails to give the object " life " will for most practical purposes have failed. The same can be said of a lighting which succeeds merely in creating a plastic impression but neglects the pictorial interpretation of the wood's intrinsic characteristics. (It must be understood, however, that this applies to those objects where the rendering of the wood-texture is the main purpose of the picture. It is obvious that when the pictorial task is the representation of an object in which the wood is incidental, the rendering of wood-grain becomes of secondary importance.)

In photographing an object we always have to aim at producing an image which shows its three-dimensional form. We know that this can only be done by creating contrasting planes of light and shadow or, in other words, by rendering the receding parts of the object in a different tone-value from that of the front parts.

These requirements tell us the principles of lighting needed here. *The basic light should be such that it does not shine " flat " on the surface, but meets it at an angle.* The angle of light-incidence must be such in relation to the angle of camera-vision that reflections are not registered by the camera. (See p. 18.)

The supplementary lighting has the task of lighting to a desired degree the shadows produced by the basic light.

A further supplementary light can be employed to create well-placed high-light effects on the edges of the object—never, however, on the flat parts of the surface.

In order to reproduce wood-grain at its best it is necessary to employ *filters* in conjunction with panchromatic emulsions. Dark mahogany requires a light red filter, light mahogany and walnut a deep orange filter, while natural oak and similar woods are sufficiently rendered with a deep-yellow filter.

POTTERY

Under this heading I include everything from earthenware to china.

With *unglazed earthenware* we must attempt to show as much of the texture as possible, and *use hard and contrasty lighting* to accentuate the feeling of " body ", so characteristic of this " masculine " material. *Supplementary lighting should be used sparingly*—an exaggerated flattening of shadow parts would defeat our purpose. We can, however, give our object a *strong highlight,* best produced by a spot-light.

In *glazed pottery* we lose the texture and rely entirely on the rendering of the reflections. Here we have to be careful. Porcelain and china are materials of a certain delicacy producing soft reflections. It is therefore wrong for the photographer to create hard, concentrated reflections. It follows that here we have to *use diffused-light sources* for the creation of our reflection effects.

Real china can be beautifully rendered by *against-the-light shots* which transmit to us the translucency of the material—*long shadows* in contrast with the delicate material enhancing its appeal.

GLASSWARE

Let me say right away that even the most experienced photographer will have his surprises every time he starts photographing a glass object. The reason for this is primarily that we have not merely to deal with reflection and absorption, as in the other branches of still-life photography, but also to cope with refraction (see p. 21). We might even have to use the refracted faculty of glass for the creation of pictorial effects.

Photographically, glass calls for more imagination than any other material; it requires not only skill, but the ability to appreciate pictorial effects quickly; this all the more because no photographer can assess the shape, structure and effect of a refracted light pattern before he actually sees it. Every glass article will reflect light in a different way—a way incalculable beforehand.

There are three ways in which we can treat glassware. First by a straightforward light and shadow treatment. Secondly by a treatment combining shadow and refraction pattern. Thirdly by means of shadow-free background photography.

The first treatment is used where we wish to show the glass in a naturalistic setting. The existence of a shadow which is linked up with the glass object helps to give the glass a certain substance and also gives, by its shape, information on the form of the glass object itself. As glassware is a material which naturally possesses a clear-cut and well-defined form, the shadow produced can also be

149

well defined. *A carbon spot-light is therefore the ideal light-source* for this type of work. The shadow should be arranged so as to avoid any undue interference with the shape of the object.

It is obvious that the production of a definite shadow demands direct lighting and that, for this reason, there must always be a certain amount of refracted light which interferes somewhere with the pictorial composition. As these refractions cannot be eliminated, the light source must be placed in such a position that the refraction comes into a part of the picture where causing least disturbance.

The second treatment aims primarily at an interesting pictorial effect, and not at a truthful rendering. The most interesting effects of combined refraction and shadow pattern can often be produced by laying the glass object on a table instead of standing it upright. *Low-angle lighting often helps the effect.*

The third treatment is, in my opinion, the most appropriate for rendering plain glassware. It is beautiful in its simplicity, and the shadow-free method enables the photographer to infuse his background with a wide range of subtle tone-values which help to give atmosphere. I have already explained the technicalities of shadow-free photography in a previous chapter (see p. 85). It is obvious that here *the basic light will not be on the object, but on the background.* It can either take the form of varying tones produced by means of light deterioration, or by more definite pattern impression produced by spotlighting.

One can help the rendering of shape by superimposing, on to the glass surface, reflections of different characters. For very deft and subtle reflections indirect lighting should be employed. For strong concentrated reflections the direct-lighting method is the appropriate one; here, however, one should again watch that the glass object is not used for the purpose of " portraying " a lamp.

SILVER AND OTHER METALS

Photographically we have to distinguish between two kinds of silver: polished silver and matt silver. Basically, both demand the same treatment— namely, *indirect lighting.*

In *polished silver* a concentrated light source, providing direct lighting, has no effect whatsoever in respect of form-rendering or tone-rendering. The only result obtained when a lamp is placed in front of a silver object is that this lamp appears in the silver as an image, in the same way as it would appear in a mirror. We thus have to *use light sources which are extended enough to avoid being reproduced in the silver surface as definite shapes.* They must appear only as a light impression of varying tone. The only light source *suitable is a paper reflector,* and the brightness of the silver's surface depends on the tone-values imposed on to the paper reflector by means of light and shadow.

It must be realised that one cannot reflect an even tone, because this would give the material a lifeless appearance, which contradicts our familiar conception of the metal, and also render the object's form insufficiently.

Naturally it is much more difficult to create good lighting for round or curved silver objects. Sometimes it is necessary to construct a "tunnel" which is indirectly illuminated and encloses the object in a half-circle.

If the paper reflectors are large enough one can put them far away from the actual object. This results, of course, in a rapid fall of the light intensity, but it gives a much greater chance to the photographer to create a wide variety of tones on the reflector.

If very intense high-lights are wanted—by means of a direct light—these *high-lights must be kept very narrow and small,* and on no account must the image of the light source appear in the object.

The lighting for *matt silver surfaces* (or pewter, aluminium, etc.) is considerably easier. The rules applying to polished silver also apply, but one has not to be quite so careful in the use of one's direct light sources for the creation of additional high-light effects.

The best *high-light effects on matt silver are produced by diffused flood-lamps using a frosted filament bulb.*

It may be necessary to differentiate in the greys of our black-and-white picture between the colours of different metals. The obvious method is by the use of a contrast filter; thus a light blue filter—or equally the use of an orthochromatic emulsion—will cause copper or brass to reproduce notably darker than silver or steel. But an exaggeration of this effect is undesirable; often a subtle difference in texture can be emphasised by the skilful arrangement of lighting.

The photography of metal objects is perhaps that branch of still-life photography requiring the greatest amount of practical knowledge and constant experiment.

PHOTOGRAPHING MACHINERY

The photographing of machinery and of technical objects generally requires certain specialised knowledge of the equipment. Such photographs can be divided into two classes: the more usual are those showing clearly the technical characteristics of the object, for reproduction in a catalogue or technical publication; but for use on the cover of a catalogue or for general non-technical applications, a certain degree of artistic licence is permissible. The engineer may deplore the results of the latter, where the advertising agent will admire them.

To consider the former case: The first essential is to ascertain from a technician exactly what features of the machine are considered of greatest importance. The camera position and lighting must then be chosen to show such parts to best advantage. Very often unrelieved front lighting will meet the requirement of realism of reproduction, since the shadows produced by side-lighting may hide important detail.

One difficulty is that of retaining the surface texture of the various metals while avoiding halation due to the catch-lights of the polished surfaces. The use of a diffuse light source leads to the loss of those finer *nuances* of texture which differentiate between polished steel, plated brass, and painted castings; a useful expedient is to give a time exposure, and to *move the principal light-source slowly during exposure in a direction parallel with the apparent movement of the principal catch-lights*—that is to say, when photographing a steel shaft the light source should move in a direction perpendicular to the shaft, or, in the case of a polished disc, the source may move circularly. The effect of such a movement can be easily studied before the exposure is made.

For the production of " arty " photographs quite different rules apply. Instead of photographing a machine with natural lighting and from a rational point of view, we can use special lighting effects and unusual camera angles. Thus, for instance, in photographing a lathe for the technical illustration of a catalogue, one would generally take it with front-lighting and with the camera roughly level. But for the impressionistic picture on the cover one would rather show a turner working on a piece of freshly machined steel between centres, the camera shooting downwards, and the work and the turner's hands lit with a hard spot-light from above.

But just as much as in the case of the realistic photograph, *soft lighting should be avoided*. Hard lighting, shadows and catch-lights as contrasty as the emulsion will stand, pin-point focus—all are essentials for the satisfactory technical photograph. Yet with either type of picture there is no objection to the photographer seeking features of aesthetic satisfaction—the curve of a casting or a stamping, the teeth of gears and the coils of springs, the shape of handles. Although their design is purely utilitarian, they may nevertheless have a beauty of their own. Machinery can supply " drama " at its best.

In photographing any type of machinery the one thing the photographer should endeavour to avoid is the need for subsequent re-touching. Yet in practically any catalogue of machinery the illustrations show little of the original photography, but are mostly produced by the air-brush. The re-toucher who can reproduce the hardness and precision of fine machinery has yet to be born, and his shortcomings are only too often apparent.

In only two directions may the re-toucher be necessary, and here it should be the aim of the photographer to minimise the need for his work: in smoothing the roughness of castings, and in painting out the background. Reference may be made to the methods of shadow-free background photography previously discussed (see p. 85).

When photographing a machine with the operator at work, one of the most common difficulties is that the operator—or generally only his hands—hides essential detail. Remember, too, that rotating machinery generally causes vibration, and even if it is desired to show the moving parts blurred, a *time exposure may lead to a blurring of the whole machine, due to vibration of the camera.*

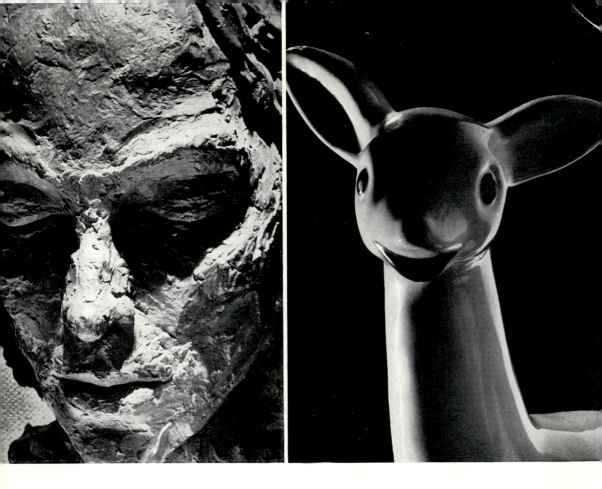

REFLECTING SURFACES IN ARTIFICIAL LIGHT.   *Left :* This clay
bust is lit in a very simple manner by a single spot light.   The
light coloured material by itself provides reflecting planes to
dilute somewhat the shadows even where they are heaviest.
Phot : *Ifor Thomas, London.*

Right : Double rim lighting is cleverly applied here to an inanimate
subject.   Phot : *Alexander, London.*

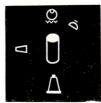

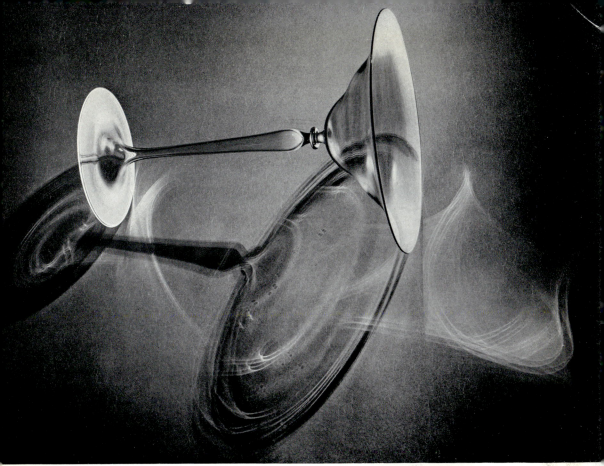

A good example of shadow and refraction treatment producing interesting patterns. It is easiest to produce this type of effect with the glass in a lying down position.   Phot : *Peterhans, Chicago.*

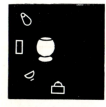

On page 154 : A straight glass photograph. The geometrical background combined with the shadow is the main composition element of the picture, while the reflection on the glass provides the material with the necessary " feel " and transparency.   Phot : *Alexander, London.*

On page 156, a single arc spot provides the shadows stressing a composition remarkable in its simplicity. Phot : *H. Althan, Stuttgart.*
On page 157 : Effect as of daylight entering through windows, but in fact produced by spot lights reaching the subject through masks shaped accordingly.   Phot : *H. Althan, Stuttgart.*

155

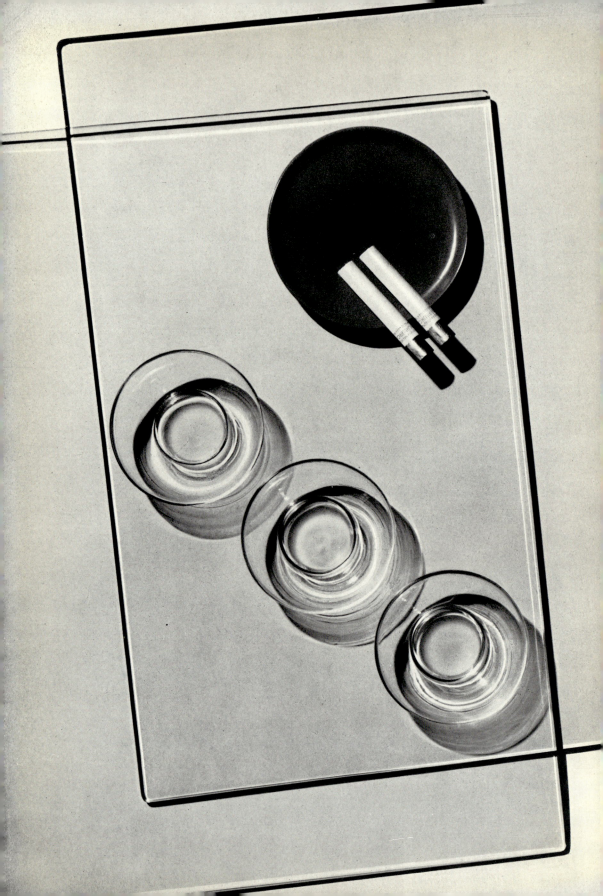

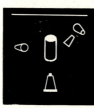

Shadow-free glass pictures. The subject placed well away from the background and separately lit. The glass effect on the bulb itself produced spots. Phot : *W. Nurnberg, London (by courtesy of General Electric).*
On page 159: Basic light : spot on background ; diffused direct lighting to produce reflections. Phot : *Alexander, London.*

Basic lighting aimed at emphasising the composition and not at rendering the surface. The spot light is therefore placed in such a position that it does not give reflections. The surface quality of the silver is rendered by purely reflected (indirect) lighting. Phot : *W. Nurnberg, London (by courtesy of Studio Ltd.).*

160

This is metal ! The photographer has achieved an unusual brightness without getting glaring high-lights. Phot : *Lazi, Stuttgart.*

161

General illumination provided by a diffused flood and a few high lights put on by a spot light from high angle. Phot : *W. G. Briggs, London.*
On page 163 : Pattern produced by low angle spot. Phot : *F. S. Lincoln.*

Ordinary electric light and flash light combined The light behind the subject helps to emphasise action. Phot : *H. Gorny, New York.* *On page 165 :* The best way of photographing smoke is to take it against the light. Long exposure is necessary to produce a smoke trail. Phot : *Knighton & Cutts, London.*

NON-PHOTOGRAPHIC LIGHT SOURCES. The problem of the inclusion of a non-photographic light source in the picture is that mostly the actual photographic lighting has to make good the insufficiency of a more primitive light. This difficulty is cleverly overcome in our example by concentrating the beam of a spot on the globe of the oil lamp. (*Courtesy of Corning Glass Works, Corning, N.Y.*).

166

On page 167, left : Supplementary lighting was necessary to equalise tone values and render detail. The halo round the candle was achieved by prolonged exposure without the flood on.   Phot: *B. Malnasy, Budapest.*

Right : The candles here have a composition value only, as the lighting on the face obviously does not originate from them. Phot : *Judith Craig, London.*

On page 168 : The main light source in this picture is obviously not the standard lamp, but photographic overhead lighting which dilutes the half-silhouette effect of the child and the shape of the lamp on the wall. Phot : *Torkel Korling, Chicago.*

167

h

CONCLUSION

There is now only one more thing I want to say, and these words are directed particularly to the beginner and the amateur.

(1) *Study people and inanimate matter* under varying lighting conditions.

(2) Realise that it is necessary to be *master of all technical means* in order to put experiences and intentions into a practical, photographic form.

(3) Do not let rules and technical knowledge influence your way of thinking, but *let your intentions govern the kind of technique you wish to employ.*

(4) *Draw inspiration from works of true art*—paintings, works of sculpture, poetry and music.

The real purpose of photography is *not to use light as a mechanical means of achieving a purely utilitarian end.* Its principal task is to create in a new form the images which denote life and everything connected with it.

On the other hand, I know from my own experience how fascinating it is to play about with artificial-light sources, and how fascinating and exciting are the experiences presented to us in such abundance by the varying conditions of light. Indeed, this thrill and fascination can be a grand stimulant to an imaginative mind and can help us to evolve ideas and to express thought-association in a pictorial form which would otherwise remain unrealised.

But there is also danger in this wealth of suggestion produced by light and shadow for our benefit. It tempts us too easily to lose ourselves in a purposeless dabbling, and it leads all too often to the achievement of nothing but shallow effects.

We have to guard ourselves against two exaggerated viewpoints—namely, to look upon artificial lighting as merely another technical means for the creation of a reproductive image, or as a cheap method for producing pictorial platitudes.

Let us remember that it is not the mere existence of light and shadow which constitutes the justification for photography, but that it is our own attitude towards light and shadow which makes photography a creative medium.

INDEX

171

172

FOCAL BOOKS ON PHOTOGRAPHY

PHOTOGRAPHING PEOPLE

By Hugo van Wadenoyen

131 photographs, 64 diagrams, 168 pages, 10 × 7 inches, cloth bound.

Price 12/6 (Postage 7d.)

Photographic portraiture has changed a lot. The technique has changed and the spirit has changed with it. The place of the painting-like solemn camera portraits has been taken by candid records of people's faces. They look casual but lively, unposed but sincere, simple but concentrated. There is purposeful craftsmanship behind the best examples. The aims, the means and the stunts of the new ways are explained in this book by a photographer who is a professional by fate and an amateur in heart.

PHOTOTIPS ON CHILDREN

By Mary and Rudolf Arnheim

83 photographs, 58 diagrammatic drawings, 112 pages, 10 × 7 inches, cloth bound.

Price 7/6 (Postage 7d.)

Photographing children seems to be not more and not less difficult than photographing anything else. But as soon as one's camera succeeds in leaving the eye-level of the grown-ups and descending to the perspective of the children, it is bound to detect a new world. The charm, the habits, the laws of this different world, all have their specific photographic aspects. General rules and small tricks mark the way to them—a way which is open to the advanced professional and amateur beginner alike.

PHOTOTIPS ON CATS AND DOGS

By Edwin Smith and Oswell Blakeston

34 photographs, 95 pages, 10 × 7 inches, cloth bound.   **Price 6/- (Postage 7d.)**

Look at the pictures in this book! Each has succeeded in snapping a pet's personality. They are quite ordinary pets like yours and mine . . . snapped with any kind of camera like yours and mine. Don't you feel tempted to have your own pictures of your own pets as brilliant as these? There is no magic about it. No complicated technique and no high-brow art rules. Some experience is all you need and this has been accumulated in these pages.

CRUISING WITH A CAMERA

By F. W. Frerk

40 photographs, 104 pages, 10 × 7 inches, cloth bound.   **Price 6/- (Postage 6d.)**

Even if you are an experienced photographer you will want to put yourself wise about photographic conditions at sea and in strange parts of the world. This book solves the technical problems in photography for the land- and seascape enthusiast. It tells you which camera to use and how—which film—which filter, and what exposure is needed in any quarter of the globe. It is written by an expert.

FOCAL BOOKS ON PHOTOGRAPHY

CAMERA TECHNIQUE

By C. I. Jacobson, Ph.D.

72 photographs, 50 diagrams, 288 pages, 7½ × 5 inches, cloth bound.

Price 10/6 (Postage 7d.)

Ways, means and effects of modern photographic technique seem endless. Success depends largely on the right choice of tools for a given purpose. The ability to judge the essential characteristics of cameras, lenses, shutters, films, filters and light sources is decisive. The necessarily critical attitude can only be built up on fundamental knowledge of the underlying principles which this book sets out to convey. It contains unbiased opinions on every possible sort of equipment with sober views on the technical rules for their use. Its sources are scientific but its purpose practical.

DEVELOPING

By C. I. Jacobson, Ph.D.

80 photographs, 70 diagrams, 288 pages, 178 formulae, 23 tables, 7½ × 5 inches, cloth bound.

Price 10/6 (Postage 7d.)

Two hundred formulae and tables in this book give a comprehensive representation of modern negative technique. Outspoken advice on their practical use and basic facts of their theoretical background will enable the photographer to think and work purposefully. The dark-room is by no means the place of secret witchcraft which some people try to make of it. Choosing the right chemicals and getting the right negative is a matter of knowledge, practice and experience, which this publication endeavours to convey in straightforward language. It will serve as a reliable source of reference for many years to come.

ENLARGING

By C. I. Jacobson and P. C. Smethurst

85 photographs, 46 diagrams, 191 pages, 7½ × 5 inches, cloth bound.

Price 7/6 (Postage 7d.)

Enlarging is more than a mechanical process. It is capable of improving the photograph and varying its effect. Individual enlarging work is based on the ability of the photographer to judge his negatives and to choose his apparatus, his paper, his chemicals. Modern materials are products of scientific research and need to be handled in accordance with its findings. Turning these into terms of practical experience, this manual offers reliable help both to professional and amateur.

MAKING COLOUR PRINTS

By Jack H. Coote

13 diagrammatic drawings, 281 pages, 7½ × 5 inches, bound. Price 5/- (Postage 5d.)

Whether you use a miniature with one of the transparency processes or whether you work with separation negatives in a studio camera, you must face the real difficulties of colour photography when thinking of paper prints. This book helps. It describes all the print-making processes in a comprehensive but simple manner, grading them according to the relative ease with which they may be worked by a newcomer to this field.

FOCAL BOOKS ON PHOTOGRAPHY

ALL THE PHOTO TRICKS

By Edwin Smith

75 photographs, 50 diagrams, 288 pages, 7½ × 5 inches, cloth bound.

Price 10/6 (Postage 7d.)

A hundred years ago photography seemed to be magic; to-day we know that it can be magic. Thousand-fold are the secrets of trick photography. Startling pictorial effects, fantastic variations of reality, amusing deceptions of the human eye and even political propaganda are worked through it. The author of this book watched for years the means and methods of photographic magicians. He is himself one of them. Freely does he give away the technique, the tricks and the ideas of a long experience.

AMATEUR PHOTOMICROGRAPHY

By Alan Jackson, B.Sc., A.I.C.

150 photographs, 50 diagrams, 160 pages, 7½ × 5 inches, bound.

Price 7/6 (Postage 6d.)

Photomicrography is as much a hobby as a scientific technique: a window into a world of fascinating forms, strangely perfect patterns composed by nature. It gives a wide view of those secrets of life which remain unseen to the naked eye. As a photographic technique, photomicrography is hardly more complicated than other camera work. It has, though, some rules of its own and it needs a few gadgets more. All this is fully explained in this book by an expert.

THE ALL-IN-ONE CAMERA BOOK

By W. Emanuel and F. L. Dash

8 colour plates, 40 photographs, 36 diagrammatic drawings, 180 pages, 7½ × 5 inches, bound.

Price 6/- (Postage 7d.)

This is a general text-book of photography: but it is different. It makes every effort to avoid presenting good photography as more difficult than it really is: a pleasant hobby with a technical background, which can be made as easy to understand fully as taking photographs itself. This book simplifies the problems without hiding them away, it emphasises the essential rules without leaving out details. Colour photography appears as a natural part of modern amateur work. This book means help and encouragement.

BETTER SNAPSHOTS—WITH ANY CAMERA

By Edwin Smith

13 photographs, 7 diagrams, 6½ × 5 inches, 52 pages.

Price 6d. (Postage 2d.)

If you have a beginner among your friends, make sure that he knows about this little book. He may decline to read " photographic literature," but he will love this modern guide at first glance. Vivid, colourful, splendidly illustrated, it gives all the necessary rules with fine examples for getting better snapshots: tells how to avoid disappointments and how to save many spools of film. You'll find it a useful pleasure to read.

FOCAL BOOKS ON PHOTOGRAPHY

THE NEW PHOTO GUIDE

to better pictures. The help and encouragement you want and just as much as you want of it. Brief, bright, bold and brilliant. You cannot go wrong with THE NEW PHOTO GUIDE. Entertainingly written and fascinatingly illustrated, each of these books tackles one subject, solves one of your problems, improves more than one of your shots. They cost only 1/6 each—and 2d. postage if you order by mail.

1. All About FOCUSING and Your Camera, by F. W. Frerk
2. All About LIGHT AND SHADE and Your Camera, by Edwin Smith
3. All About FILTERS and Your Camera, by C. I. Jacobson
4. All About PORTRAITS and Your Camera, by Hugo van Wadenoyen
5. All About EXPOSURE and Your Camera, by C. I. Jacobson
6. All About THE RIGHT MOMENT and Your Camera, by Alex. Strasser
7. All About LAND, SEA, SKY and Your Camera, by Hugo van Wadenoyen
8. All About FORMULAE in Your Darkroom, by C. I. Jacobson
9. All About DAYLIGHT INDOORS and Your Camera, by Hugo van Wadenoyen
10. All About IMPROVING NEGATIVES, by F. W. Frerk
11. All About WINTER PHOTOGRAPHY and Your Camera, by Edwin Smith
12. All About TRACING TROUBLES in Your Photographs, by A. Merryweather
13. All About ONE LAMP ONLY and Your Camera, by Hugo van Wadenoyen
14. All About THE SECOND LAMP and Your Camera, by Hugo van Wadenoyen
15. All About COMPOSITION and Your Camera, by A. Kraszna-Krausz
16. All About BETTER PRINTS in Your Darkroom, by F. W. Frerk

Edited by A. KRASZNA-KRAUSZ

And if you have any difficulty or think you have made a mistake, drop a line to
FOCAL PRESS LTD., 31, FITZROY SQUARE, LONDON, W.1.
We shall be glad to help you—free of charge of course. But matters will be simpler for us if you enclose a stamped and addressed envelope for our answer.